Praise for *Beyond the 401(k)*

"This book is an indispensable guide for wealth managers and financial advisors. It's packed with useful ideas, strategies and concrete examples of how Cash Balance Plans can make a tremendous impact on your clients' businesses as well as your own. The authors provide simple and clear explanations, demystifying these complex plans, so you'll feel confident presenting the concept to clients.

This book should be required reading for any advisor working with high net worth clients and successful business owners. Offering Cash Balance Plans as an option to my clients has enhanced my wealth management practice and given me a strong competitive edge. I've been able to help many clients dramatically improve their overall retirement planning and accelerate pre-tax savings.

If you intend to be regarded as an expert in the area of retirement plans, this book is essential to your practice."

— *Todd Feltz, President, Feltz WealthPLAN, Barron's Top 100 Independent Advisors in America*

"*Beyond the 401(k)* is an essential guide to Cash Balance Plans, and a highly valuable tool for advisors who want to grow their retirement plan businesses. This book explains and educates; it is both practical and technically correct. The book walks the reader through the right way to set up and operate a Cash Balance Plan, and gives practical answers to the questions often asked. The lessons in this book should be committed to memory, since they are the keys to successfully working with business owners and professionals."

— *Fred Reish, ERISA Attorney, nationally acclaimed retirement plan expert recognized as "The 401(k) Industry's Most Influential Person"*

"You can't afford not to read this book. Dan Kravitz and his team will open your eyes and change your thinking about retirement and tax planning opportunities. If you're not already introducing Cash Balance Plans to your clients, they may be missing out on one of the best tax savings and retirement vehicles around today.

Beyond the 401(k) is the clearest and most helpful explanation of Cash Balance Plans I've read. It offers a complete roadmap to growing your business using these unique tax-favored hybrid plans, written by a national leader who is backed by a team of sophisticated technical professionals."

— *David Roberts, CPA, Managing Partner*
RBZ Certified Public Accountants & Strategic Business Consultants

"Small business owners face a variety of unique challenges and demands related to retirement planning. Cash Balance Plans, along with a variety of other advanced retirement plan designs, can provide meaningful solutions to these problems, allowing business owners to defer more toward retirement while reducing their current tax liabilities.

Beyond the 401(k) simplifies the discussion of these issues and opportunities with an approachability and insight that is grounded in deep experience. It is a valuable resource for financial professionals."

— *E. Thomas Foster Jr., JD*
Vice President and National Spokesperson for
The Hartford's retirement plans

"The knowledge and tools in this book have opened many new doors for my TPA firm. There is simply no more powerful tool for saving a large amount of federal taxes and accumulating enormous amounts of savings for retirement in a short period of time, on a tax-deductible basis, than by using a Cash Balance Plan.

The team at Kravitz has made this plan type the primary focus of their practice, and this book is an opportunity to learn from their expertise. Because of the unique aspects of this hybrid plan, there are few firms we would trust to do this work, from plan design to investments and administration. Promoting Cash Balance Plans to our clients has been a huge value-add and it helps advisors as well, who may also secure the 401(k) plan in the process.

To TPA and CPA practices everywhere who don't have the expertise in-house, learning from this book and partnering with Kravitz is your answer to tapping into successful business owners."

— *Tom Lastuvka, QKA, Co-founder*
Qualified Plan Consultants

How Financial Advisors Can Grow Their Businesses with **Cash Balance Plans**

BEYOND THE 401(k)

DANIEL KRAVITZ, KEN GUIDROZ
& STEVEN SANSONE

www.CashBalanceBook.com

Beyond the 401(k): How Financial Advisors Can Grow Their Businesses with Cash Balance Plans

For information about this title, and information about special discounts for bulk purchases, please contact Kravitz Publishing:

15760 Ventura Blvd., Suite 910
Encino, CA 91436
(818) 995-6100
(877) CB-Plans
books@kravitzinc.com

Library of Congress Cataloging-In-Publication Data is available.

ISBN-13: 978-0-9828730-0-7
ISBN-10: 0-9828-7300-X

Printed in the United States of America

Cover design by Rigney Graphics
Interior design by 1106 Design

Kravitz is the marketing name for the businesses of Kravitz, Inc. and Kravitz Investment Services, Inc. Kravitz, Inc. provides actuarial and consulting advice on the design and administration of retirement plans. Kravitz Investment Services, Inc. is a registered investment advisory firm that provides investment advice and asset management.

Table of Contents

Foreword

By Fred Reish

As this book is being written, America's business owners and professionals are facing a retirement crisis. How do they save enough to maintain their standards of living in retirement, given the limits of 401(k) plans? Many rank-and-file employees may be able to cope, considering their Social Security retirement benefits in combination with 401(k) savings. However, there are few options available to business owners and professionals other than the inefficient approach of after-tax savings.

This book, written by key members of the Kravitz organization, discusses what is perhaps the best of those limited options: Cash Balance Plans.

However, business owners and professionals need to rely on their advisors to explain Cash Balance Plans and to help them find experienced consultants and administrators. Cash Balance Plans need to be designed, administered, and invested in a sophisticated and knowledgeable way; it takes experience to do that.

Let me explain my thinking. At this time, our country is facing a number of significant retirement issues, including the following:

- **Aging Baby Boomers.** America's largest generation is rapidly approaching retirement, and it's no secret that the Boomers are poorly prepared. For those who earn enough to save more, the situation can be remedied, but for most it will mean working longer, perhaps well into their 70s.

- **Increasing income tax rates are a virtual certainty.** First, the rates will effectively increase due to the lapse of the Bush tax cuts. Second, there may be additional increases to help fund the large deficits being incurred by state and federal governments. Regardless of the cause or the timing, it seems virtually certain that business owners and professionals will be paying a larger share of their incomes to the government. As a result, they will have less to save from their remaining after-tax income. It is important that they find before-tax savings vehicles.
- **Deferral limits for 401(k) plans are so low that they're of limited value to high income earners.** Even when a 401(k) plan is properly designed for professional firms, closely-held corporations and family-owned businesses—with cross-tested contributions—owners can accumulate only about $50,000 per year. Most experts recommend that investors withdraw no more than 4% to 5% of their investments each year in retirement, and that means that a million dollar 401(k) account balance would support only $40,000 to $50,000 a year of income. Even when combined with Social Security, that's significantly less than what most business owners and professionals will need to maintain their standard of living in retirement.
- **Prudent investing alone cannot solve the problem.** Business owners and professionals are, more and more, turning to their investment advisors and financial advisors for help with investing and saving for retirement. However, after-tax saving is an inefficient way of achieving the goal. As a result, advisors need tax-efficient ways to help their clients save significant amounts of money over relatively short periods of time.

What should business owners and professionals do?

Cross-tested 401(k) plans are the first step, the foundation that enables them to accumulate significant amounts. That's the starting point, but it is not enough.

In appropriate situations, the second step is to design and adopt a Cash Balance Plan. The criteria for determining whether a Cash Balance Plan is appropriate for a given organization are described in this book.

While Cash Balance Plans are effective tools for accumulating substantial amounts over relatively short periods of time, they are also defined benefit pension plans, which means that there is a degree of complexity. As a result, a poorly designed Cash Balance Plan can be a serious problem. A poorly administered or invested Cash Balance Plan can present significant operational issues and client disappointment.

An aggressively invested Cash Balance Plan can result in excess assets in good years, with the potential of substantial taxes in reversions if the plan is terminated. In bad years, the possibility of underfunding presents a different host of problems, including required additional contributions during hard times. As a result, investments and their allocations need to be specially and thoughtfully designed for a Cash Balance Plan.

These issues and challenges are addressed throughout this book. The authors discuss the advantages of properly designing, administering and investing Cash Balance Plans and also warn the reader about the downside of mistakes in all three of those areas. Those lessons should be committed to memory by the reader, since they are keys to successfully working with business owners and professionals, both at the beginning—the design and installation stage—and along the way, during the administration and investing stages. Done properly, Cash Balance Plans will accomplish the goals of the plan sponsors; done improperly, they will be expensive and frustrating.

This book explains and educates; it is both practical and technically correct. The book walks the reader through the right way to set up and operate a Cash Balance Plan, and gives practical answers to the questions often asked about these plans. The authors also bring clarity to the misunderstandings that abound about Cash Balance Plans. The information in this book is a valuable tool for helping advisers accomplish their clients' retirement goals.

Fred Reish *is one of the nation's leading ERISA attorneys and a widely cited expert on retirement plans and employee benefits. He was named one of "15 Legends in the Development of Retirement Plans" by* PLANSPONSOR *magazine and honored as the 401(k) Industry's Most Influential Person by 401(k) Wire, along with numerous other industry awards. He has been recognized in the legal community as one of "The Best Lawyers in America," and as a "Super Lawyer in Southern California." He is regularly quoted in pension publications and national media, and has written four books and more than 350 articles about retirement plans.*

Introduction:

How Reading this Book Can Transform Your Business

We wrote this book with one goal in mind: to help financial advisors gain a competitive edge using Cash Balance Plans. You'll learn how to help your clients move beyond the 401(k) to accelerate retirement savings, reduce taxes, and deliver better benefits for employees.

A Cash Balance Plan is a unique type of IRS-qualified retirement plan also known as a hybrid plan, since it features characteristics of both defined benefit and defined contribution plans. Compared with a 401(k), a Cash Balance Plan allows for significantly larger contributions, generally increasing based on a participant's age. These plans can help business owners catch up on delayed savings, recoup market losses, and save on taxes.

Despite their many advantages, Cash Balance Plans are not nearly as well known or understood as 401(k) plans. One reason is that they haven't been around as long, and another is that they require the certification of an enrolled actuary. As a result, many advisors and their clients have been missing out on a highly valuable financial planning opportunity. *Beyond the 401(k)* is your step-by-step guide to understanding and marketing Cash Balance Plans.

Most retirement professionals agree that the 401(k) has become a mass market commodity, and that sales pitches for 401(k) plans frequently sound alike. Cash Balance Plans offer a way to stand out from the crowd, since relatively few advisors have the awareness and knowledge to present these plans to their clients. Most business owners are unaware that they can put away large sums for retirement, reduce taxes and help their employees at the same time.

Not only are these unique hybrid plans a smart way to differentiate yourself as an advisor, they can also open the door to new 401(k) and wealth management business. Many advisors we've worked with through our Cash Balance Coach® program have won new 401(k) business along with Cash Balance Plan sales.

Of course, Cash Balance Plans are not a fit for every client. Advisors need to know when and where these advanced plans make sense. Because a Cash Balance Plan is a defined benefit pension plan with mandatory annual contributions, consistent cash flow and consistent profit patterns are very important.

Reading this book will empower you with an understanding of the essentials of Cash Balance Plans, so you can share the opportunity with clients in an informed, intelligent manner. You'll be able to help your clients accelerate retirement savings and reduce their tax obligations—you'll be able to take them *Beyond the 401(k).*

What you'll learn:

Chapter 1 reveals the results of years of research on retirement planning errors in hundreds of companies across the country. We've summarized them in a list called "The 10 Biggest Retirement Mistakes that High Income Professionals and Business Owners Make." You'll learn how to help your clients avoid them.

Chapter 2 is a consideration of how Cash Balance Plans enhance 401(k) plans, allowing for accelerated savings and greater tax deferral. This chapter gives you a helpful overview of plan basics through informative case studies, and highlights the top five advantages of Cash Balance Plans.

Chapter 3 explains how Cash Balance Plans can be a powerful tool for recruiting and retaining top talent in an increasingly competitive global economy. We'll take a closer look at some of the most compelling features of Cash Balance Plans that appeal to high income earners and employees at all levels of a company.

Chapter 4 is an in-depth look at the investment side of Cash Balance Plans, which require a very different strategy from 401(k)s or traditional defined benefit plans. You'll learn the seven fundamental investment principles that shape an effective strategy, and why they make a big difference to the plan's success.

Chapter 5 takes a close-up look at some of the misinformation floating around about Cash Balance Plans. We separate the myths from the facts, so you'll be ready to answer tough questions and objections. We also look at the advantages of Cash Balance over traditional defined benefit plans.

Chapter 6 introduces you to some of the key factors involved in plan design, including satisfying IRS nondiscrimination testing, meeting participation requirements and providing "meaningful benefits" to employees. We also explain the basics of plan funding and allocation.

Chapter 7 teaches you how to succeed in the increasingly noisy and competitive retirement plan marketplace. Learn how to use the Cash Balance opportunity to open doors using direct marketing, niche marketing, networking with CPAs, and setting up speaking engagements. We'll show you how to evaluate potential clients and convert Cash Balance leads into sales.

Chapter 8 takes a look at Cash Balance Plans in the context of the historical evolution of pensions. Two key dates stand out in the timeline. The first is 1985, when Bank of America adopted the first Cash Balance Plan and the second is 2006, when the Pension Protection Act clarified the legality of Cash Balance Plans and allowed for larger tax deductible contributions.

Chapter 9 tests what you've learned after reading this book, challenging you with a Cash Balance Plan quiz. From plan basics to investment options, from participation levels to the PBGC, these 20 questions will get you thinking and you'll feel well prepared to confidently present the Cash Balance opportunity to prospects.

Chapter 10 is a helpful wrap-up and reference guide, with seven handy checklists for advisors. Who are the top 10 candidates for Cash Balance Plans? What information should you gather from potential clients? This chapter is a guide you'll refer to again and again as you grow your retirement plan business in the coming years.

Important Caveat For Advisors

While this book will help improve your retirement planning knowledge and will teach you how to market Cash Balance Plans, the information here is of a general nature and is not intended as legal, actuarial or accounting advice. Nor is this book a substitute for getting specific advice from an attorney, actuary or CPA on your client's particular situation. With that caution in mind, let's begin our exploration of Cash Balance Plans.

1

The 10 Biggest Retirement Mistakes that High Income Professionals and Business Owners Make

Whose fault is it when an attorney has a successful practice but little to show for it when it comes time to retire? Who's responsible when the owner of a highly profitable business doesn't know how to squeeze 20 years of retirement savings into 10? Who's to blame when a sole proprietor making $250,000 a year retires but can't maintain her lifestyle because of low retirement plan contribution limits?

Drawing on decades of experience, we concluded that the blame lies partly with retirement advisors and partly with business owners themselves. The good news is that Cash Balance Plans can help your clients avoid many retirement planning blunders.

Our research focused on more than 300 companies for which we've created Cash Balance Plans during the past 20 years. We identified the most common retirement mistakes made by the following types of clients:

- Highly profitable companies of all types and sizes
- Family businesses
- Closely-held businesses

- Law firms of all sizes
- Medical groups of all sizes
- Professional firms of all types, including CPAs, engineers, and architects
- Companies with older owners who have delayed saving for retirement
- Business owners who highly value asset protection
- Companies seeking enhanced benefits packages for staff
- Sole proprietorships with incomes exceeding $250,000 per year

Through the course of our analysis, we consistently saw retirement savings falling far short of retirement income goals. We wanted to understand why.

Our research included analyzing the retirement planning practices in place at these companies prior to their engagement with Kravitz. We discovered that almost every organization made the same mistakes, over and over again.

The Top 10 Mistakes

We believe that for advisors to help make things go right, they must first understand what's going wrong. The 10 most frequent retirement planning mistakes made by high income professionals and business owners, in reverse rank order, were:

10. **Relied on bad advice about IRS 401(k) rules.** A little knowledge can be a dangerous thing, especially if you're willing to share it. In 15% of the companies we examined, we saw reliance on advice from uninformed colleagues or advisors. Many partners and professionals had never heard that Cash Balance Plans can be added on to existing 401(k) Profit Sharing plans as an IRS-approved way to increase contributions to retirement accounts.

9. **Left retirement plan decisions to Human Resources executives.** Successful business owners are busy people who have learned to delegate to get ahead. In 15% of companies, retirement plan decisions were delegated to the head of human resources. HR people typically view 401(k) plans as a commodity and their objective is to minimize costs, rather than maximize retirement savings opportunities for owners and staff.

8. **Resisted spending money to set up a tax-efficient plan.** There's a saying in the investment world, "It's not the fee that counts, but the overall return." In 17% of the companies we studied, there was a penny-wise, pound-foolish mentality. People resisted the cost of setting up a plan, even though it would deliver significant tax savings down the road.

7. **Overestimated their own ability to handle investments.** Sometimes being smart can be a liability. In 18% of the companies we examined, owners and partners tried making their own investment decisions, often running into major problems. As the book *Why Smart People Make Big Money Mistakes* asks, why do so many otherwise rational individuals make irrational decisions when it comes to money?

6. **Feared any plan that gave more money to employees.** Some business owners assume that any plan that gives more money to employees is the wrong way to go. In 26% of the companies we reviewed, owners held back out of fear of increasing payments to employees. However, those fears are usually overcome when business owners see how Cash Balance Plans can be leveraged for accelerated retirement savings, tax benefits and employee retention opportunities.

5. **Thought pre-tax savings were not as beneficial as after-tax savings.** Not everyone is willing to do the math. In 29% of the companies examined, there was a common miscalculation about the accumulated

benefits of after-tax savings. Some owners assume that it's better to bite the bullet and pay taxes now rather than later. Cash Balance Plans are part of a category called "qualified plans," indicating their tax-favored status with the IRS. Tax advisors generally agree that these plans should be funded to their maximum before other strategies are explored.

4. **Kept all assets tied up in the business.** Growing a business can really drain resources. In 31% of the companies studied, the owners believed in pouring profits back into the company. For many, this investment strategy seemed to offer the highest rate of return. However, this tied up all of their assets in the company, which is a vulnerable strategy when it comes to retirement. Many ended up with no assets safe from creditors in the event of business failure.

3. **Assumed advanced plans were too good to be true.** Many people accept the old adage that if something sounds too good to be true, it is. In 35% of the companies we examined there was healthy skepticism about plans that allowed accelerated savings. Partners and owners over age 40 who needed to "catch-up" on their retirement savings were eager to learn the truth about plans with age-dependent contributions. In fact, it's true: the older you are, the faster you can accelerate retirement savings in a Cash Balance Plan.

2. **Thought the IRS qualified plan limit was $16,500.** Let's face it, few people enjoy digging deep into IRS regulations. Owners at 38% of the companies in our study believed that $16,500 was the IRS limit in all cases. Most were surprised to learn that by adding a Cash Balance Plan to an existing 401(k) Profit Sharing plan they could significantly increase pre-tax contributions, sometimes as much as $100,000 to $200,000 annually

1. **Started saving for retirement too late, or didn't save enough.** Delayed and insufficient savings was the number one problem we discovered. It was a critical issue for 49% of the companies we studied. Many professionals and entrepreneurs neglect their personal retirement savings while building their practice or their company. Consequently they needed to catch up on their retirement savings, trying to compress 20+ years of savings into 10 years or less.

By reading *Beyond the 401(k)*, you've taken an important step toward preventing or remedying many of these common mistakes. You have the opportunity to make a major impact on your clients' long-term financial security, help them recover from past retirement planning errors and make up for lost time. The more you know about Cash Balance Plans, the better you'll be able to serve key high income professionals, business owners and their employees. Keep reading.

2

How Cash Balance Plans Enhance the 401(k)

Like many physicians, Dr. Vanessa Holmes[1] was worried sick about retirement. As the pension committee chairperson of Summit Medical Group, she was accountable to more than 200 doctors, so her anxiety about retirement savings was multiplied 200-fold. Dr. Holmes and her colleagues urgently needed to catch up on creating healthy retirement portfolios. After the high costs of medical school, residency, and establishing a practice, little remained for retirement savings in the first half of their careers.

Now in their 40s and 50s, these physicians had more money to put aside, but taxes took a huge bite and low 401(k) contribution limits made it hard to save aggressively.

Consider the case of an obstetrician in the group, Dr. William Alvarado. If you faced a complicated pregnancy, you would want him as your doctor. Dr. Alvarado, who lost his own mother at a young age, had an incredible bedside manner and was always reassuring to expectant parents. Although he was on call day and night, he never resented those after-midnight deliveries because all he ever wanted to do was become

[1] *Case studies in this book are based on actual Kravitz clients, but all names and identifying details of companies and individuals have been changed to protect their privacy.*

a doctor. The son of a truck driver, he had worked his way through college and borrowed heavily to get through medical school. Finally, after decades of hard work, Dr. Alvarado had the cash flow to repay his loans, pay the steep malpractice insurance required of an obstetrician, and join a leading medical group.

As a doctor in his late 40s, he was turning the corner financially and making the healthy income needed to put his children through college. It was time to start saving for the retirement he and his wife had dreamed about, which included money for traveling and spoiling their future grandchildren. But then the dilemma hit: taxes consumed a lot of his income and he was only able to save $49,000 annually in his 401(k) Profit Sharing plan. Dr. Alvarado worried that he would never be able to save enough in his remaining working years to make those retirement dreams a reality.

A solution to this retirement dilemma soon arrived: Dr. Holmes and the pension committee added a Cash Balance Plan to Summit Medical Group's existing 401(k) Profit Sharing plan. The new Cash Balance Plan more than doubled contribution amounts for many physicians. As you can see in the following Contribution Limits Table, Cash Balance limits are significantly higher, and they increase based on participants' ages.

Contribution Limits

401(k) Profit Sharing & Cash Balance Plans

Age	401(k) Only	401(k) with Profit Sharing	Cash Balance	Total	Tax savings*
60-65	$22,000	$54,500	$209,000	**$263,500**	$105,400
55-59	$22,000	$54,500	$164,000	**$218,500**	$87,400
50-54	$22,000	$54,500	$125,000	**$179,500**	$71,800
45-49	$16,500	$49,000	$96,000	**$145,000**	$58,000
40-44	$16,500	$49,000	$73,000	**$122,000**	$48,800
35-39	$16,500	$49,000	$56,000	**$105,000**	$42,000
30-34	$16,500	$49,000	$43,000	**$92,000**	$36,800

**Assuming 40% tax bracket, taxes are deferred.*

"I've noticed that around 40 years of age the group's retirement plan becomes a huge issue for the doctors," said Dr. Holmes. "Our physicians are now able to have the medical group contribute an additional $30,000 to $85,000 on top of the $49,000 they were saving in our 401(k) Profit Sharing Plan. Because Cash Balance Plans permit age-graduated contributions, some doctors over 50 received contributions in excess of $150,000, while some doctors in their 60s got over $200,000 a year."

A Cash Balance Plan solved the biggest retirement challenge for Summit Medical Group, and for so many other organizations we work with. Beyond the medical community, countless small business owners and highly compensated professionals are desperate to accelerate their retirement savings. Cash Balance Plans are often the ideal solution. Fortunately, recent legislative changes are encouraging many more successful business owners and partners to adopt Cash Balance Plans to supplement their existing 401(k) plans.

What is a Cash Balance Plan?

A Cash Balance Plan is a qualified (tax-favored) retirement plan that combines the high contribution amounts of a defined benefit plan with the look, feel and portability of a defined contribution plan. For that reason, it's part of a category called "hybrid" plans. Cash Balance Plans resemble 401(k) plans in terms of offering individual, portable retirement accounts. But they allow significantly higher contribution levels and use different investment principles.

In a Cash Balance Plan, each participant has an account that grows annually in two ways: first, with an employer contribution and second, with an interest credit on previous contributions.

The employer contribution is determined by a formula specified in the plan document, and can be either a percentage of pay, a flat dollar amount or a combination of the two.

The annual interest credit is guaranteed and is not dependent on the plan's investment performance. The interest credit is usually tied to a benchmark such as the 30-year Treasury Securities Interest Rate, which has averaged around 4% to 5% in recent years.

When a participant terminates employment, he or she is eligible to receive the vested portion of the Cash Balance account balance as a lump sum or as an annuity. The Cash Balance account can be rolled over into an IRA or another qualified retirement plan if the participant wishes to continue deferring taxes.

Pension 101: Definitions

Defined Benefit Plan: A pension plan which gives an employee a specific monthly or annual benefit, usually based on salary history and/or years of service. The employer contributes to the plan and the employer bears the investment risk.

Defined Contribution Plan: A retirement plan which may allow employees to contribute portions of their salaries to individual retirement accounts within the plan. Employers may match a portion of the contributions, but employees bear the investment risk. Examples are a 401(k) plan, a 403(b) plan and a SEP.

Qualified Plan: A plan that receives favorable tax treatment by the IRS and offers a variety of tax benefits for employers. Cash Balance and 401(k) plans are both examples of qualified plans, because they meet the requirements of Internal Revenue Code Section 401(a) and the Employee Retirement Income Security Act of 1974 (ERISA). Contributions to qualified plans are tax-deferred until withdrawn by participants.

How are Cash Balance Plan Investments Handled?

Cash Balance Plan assets are pooled and invested collectively by the trustee or investment manager, with the goal of meeting the guaranteed interest crediting rate (ICR) written into the plan document. If the plan's investment earnings exceed the guaranteed rate, the excess will be used to reduce future employer contributions. This will not affect the amount credited to participants' accounts. That is, the account will increase according to the plan's schedule and the increases will be funded partly from a reduced employer contribution and partly from the excess investment earnings.

Conversely, if the plan's investment earnings are less than the guaranteed interest crediting rate, then future employer contributions must increase to make up for the shortfall. This make-up contribution can be spread over seven years if necessary, although we generally don't recommend it. These issues are covered in detail in Chapter 4 of this book.

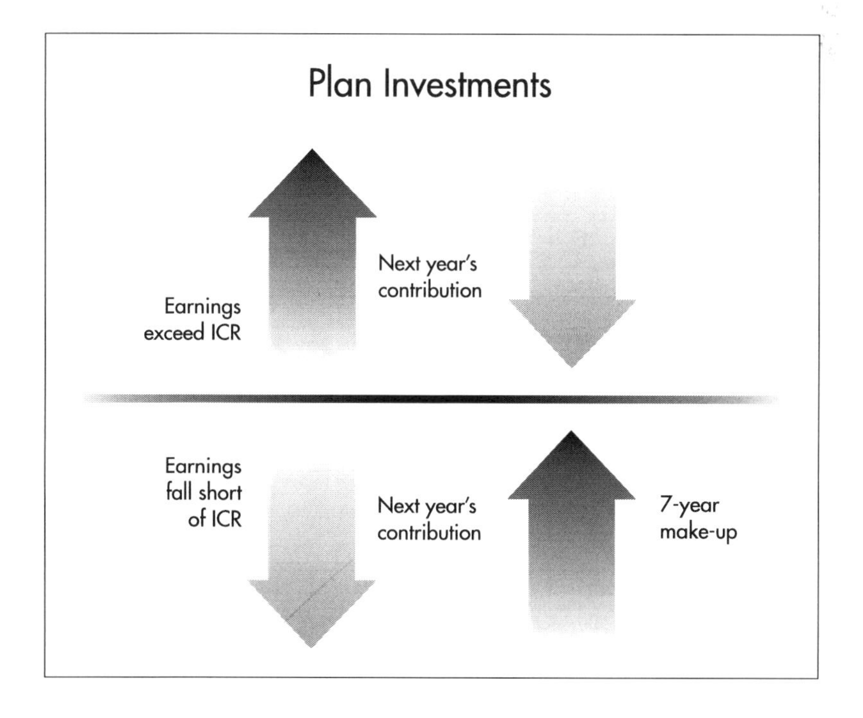

Plan sponsors can choose from a wide range of investment vehicles to meet the targeted interest crediting rate (ICR). The most widely used ICR is the 30-year Treasury Securities Interest Rate, chosen by a majority of Cash Balance Plan sponsors for reasons discussed in Chapter 4 of this book. The rate is calculated based on the average of the daily yield on the 30-year US Treasury Bond during December of the previous year.

The investment goal of any Cash Balance Plan is to achieve performance as close to the ICR as possible, since deviation creates uncertainty for future contributions.

Can Cash Balance Plans be Offered in Addition to Other Plans?

Yes, employers can offer a combination of qualified retirement plans in order to maximize contribution amounts. In most cases, a Cash Balance Plan is set up in conjunction with a 401(k) Profit Sharing plan to produce the desired contribution levels.

How Flexible are Cash Balance Plans?

During the plan design stage, there is great flexibility for varying contribution levels and participation in a Cash Balance Plan, as long as it passes nondiscrimination testing (see Chapter 6 for an overview of testing). This flexibility is one of many reasons why the plans work so well for firms with multiple owners or partners.

Everyone does not need to participate equally in a Cash Balance Plan, and some partners can be excluded from the plan. Contribution amounts can be set as a percentage of pay, a flat dollar amount or a combination of the two, and each participant can have a different contribution amount. Once determined, these contribution amounts become part of the plan document.

However, the plan document can be amended periodically if an employer needs to change these contribution amounts. Any reductions must be made before an employee works 1,000 hours during a plan year.

For contribution increases, the plan must be amended within two and a half months following the end of a plan year or pass nondiscrimination testing on its own.

What About Tax Deductions and the IRS?

As a qualified plan with preferred tax status, a Cash Balance Plan allows business owners a tax deduction for all contributions made on behalf of themselves and their employees. Corporations deduct the entire contribution on their corporate tax return. Businesses taxed as sole proprietorships or partnerships deduct the non-owner portions on their business tax return, and the portions attributable to owners on the owner's personal tax return (similar to 401(k) deferrals).

The partnership's agreement must define the method of allocation among the partners. Most partnerships that adopt Cash Balance Plans don't want the partners' contributions allocated in the same manner as other firm expenses, in proportion to ownership.

After consulting with the firm's attorney and tax advisor, partnerships should have an agreement to assure that each partner is allocated an appropriate share of the Cash Balance Plan's cost.

Like any other qualified plan, a Cash Balance Plan is subject to IRS nondiscrimination testing. Employers can generally anticipate contributions in the range of 5% to 7.5% of pay for staff if the owners or partners receive the maximum Cash Balance contribution. The exact amount depends on a number of factors including, but not limited to, the number of employees meeting minimum eligibility, their age, and their pay, as well as the minimums and maximums the government has set. The process of determining this amount is what we call nondiscrimination testing. Most plans will have an annual nondiscrimination test prepared to ensure that all IRS rules are being followed, allowing the plan to maintain its tax-qualified status. Chapter 6 of this book discusses testing and compliance in more detail.

Sample Cash Balance Plan

	Age	401(k)	Profit Sharing	Cash Balance	Total Contribution	Tax Savings*
Owners						
1	61	$22,000	$32,500	$224,000	**$278,500**	$111,400
2	58	$22,000	$32,500	$190,000	**$244,500**	$97,800
3	50	$22,000	$32,500	$124,000	**$178,500**	$71,400
4	42	$16,500	$32,500	$81,000	**$130,000**	$52,000
5	36	$16,500	$32,500	$58,000	**$107,000**	$42,800
Subtotal		**$99,000**	**$162,500**	**$677,000**	**$938,500**	**$375,400**
			7.5% of pay	*$1,000 each*		
22 Employees			$74,250	$22,000	**$96,250**	$38,500
Total					**$1,034,750**	$413,900
				Percent to Owners:	**91%**	

**Assuming 40% tax bracket; taxes are deferred.*

Naturally, it's more expensive to set up and maintain a Cash Balance Plan than a 401(k) Profit Sharing plan because the plan requires the expertise of an actuary. Expenses vary based on the size of the plan and the annual testing requirements, but not paying the extra cost could be a poor business decision. Ultimately, once a Cash Balance study is prepared, it becomes a relatively simple math equation to compare the plan's costs with the financial benefits.

The sample illustration above shows in concrete terms the bottom-line impact of adding a Cash Balance Plan for a small business with five owners and 22 employees. Tax savings of more than $400,000 a year, an enhanced employee benefit program, and dramatically accelerated retirement savings for the owners easily offset the administrative costs.

Lawyers Also Need to Exceed Savings Speed Limits

The body of evidence proves, without a shadow of a doubt, that law firms can benefit greatly from Cash Balance Plans.

Consider the case of Caroline Barclay, a family law attorney and a partner at Spenser, Shaw & Ellis. Perhaps the reason Caroline was so empathetic to her clients going through divorce was the fact that she had been there herself. As a mother of two boys, she was working part time as an attorney to supplement the family income. When her marriage ended suddenly, she was left as the sole breadwinner. She took quick steps to double her income.

Raising two boys while paying off her college and law school loans was an expensive proposition, but Caroline always put the welfare of her clients first. She talked many potential clients out of divorce and got them in to marriage counseling instead. She showed others the advantages of a mediated divorce at one-tenth the cost of litigation. But for others who needed her on their side at $450 an hour, she actually loved to go to court and fight for child custody or a fair settlement.

But life didn't seem fair to Caroline as she reached middle age. She was a valued partner at her law firm and money was finally coming in, but how could she put away enough for retirement with low 401(k) limits and a major tax bite out of her income? Financial advice books and magazines scolded her for not starting to save at a younger age, but that just wasn't an option for her.

To make matters worse, the stock market plunges of 2000 and 2008 had hit her retirement savings hard. Caroline would wake up in the middle of the night and couldn't get back to sleep because of the nagging doubt—will I have enough money to make it through retirement?

For lawyers like Carolyn Barclay and her partners, there is an answer.

"Having worked with many law firms, I've found them eager to find ways to reduce their tax burdens," said David Roberts, a CPA with the Los Angeles firm RBZ. "One of the most significant methods I've seen them use is implementing a Cash Balance Pension Plan in addition to their 401(k) Profit Sharing plan. This allows them to dramatically increase pre-tax contributions to qualified plans, sometimes as high as $200,000 per year. Cash Balance is a complex plan that may not be right for everyone, but for those who can, I would strongly recommend that they look closely at the option."

Another law firm case study illustrates David Roberts' point: a 75-attorney firm in Los Angeles was hit hard by the bear market of 2000–2002. Many partners saw their 401(k) assets drop by 50% to 75% in value. While they learned a lifetime lesson in asset allocation and diversification, they nonetheless needed to make up those losses over the ensuing years.

They chose to add a Cash Balance Plan to their existing 401(k) plan, which allowed them to make significant "catch-up" contributions. Within four years, many saw their retirement accounts surpass 1999 highs by a significant amount.

Not only have their accounts caught up, but many of their assets are now in conservatively managed Cash Balance accounts, protected from dramatic market declines.

In another example, several senior partners in a Los Angeles law firm were participants in a $2 million unfunded deferred compensation program. This program was a significant liability to the firm because it provided no tax deduction and offered its participants no protection from creditors. Additionally, the other partners in the firm wanted to be included in a retirement program.

Kravitz stepped in and designed a Cash Balance Plan that included all partners. The two name partners were made whole after several years of contributions to the plan, which at their ages was approximately $200,000 per year. The other partners received significant contributions to their accounts as well.

The program has gone so well that it's now mandatory for all partners to get a Cash Balance contribution, so that all of them "will be able to retire at 65 and not be forced to continue working."

With close to 200 law firm clients, Kravitz has been able to help many partners accelerate their retirement savings and increase their tax

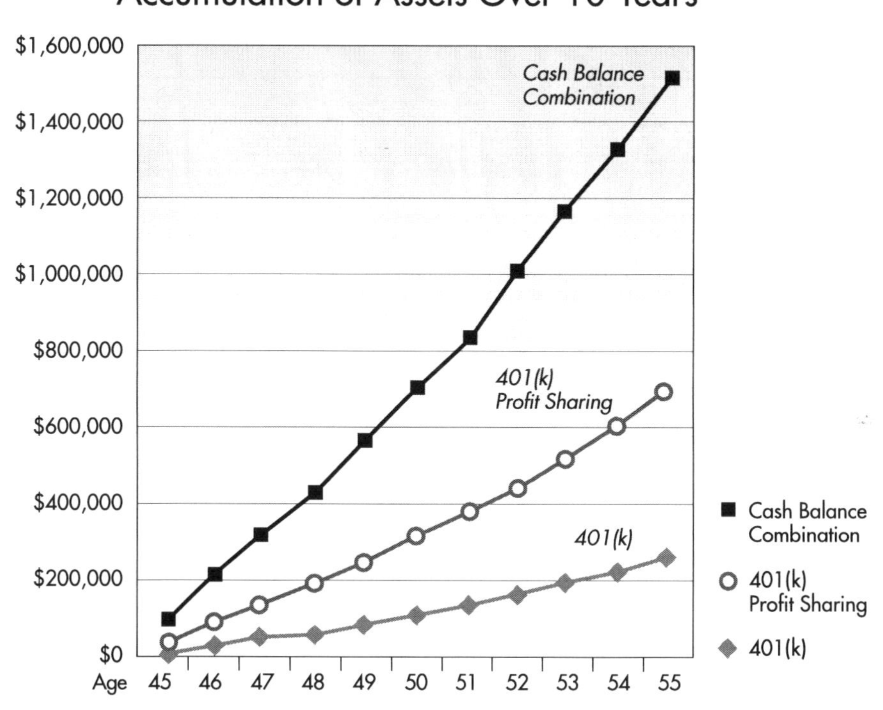

deductions while adding an employee benefit that helps attract and reward key staff. The table above illustrates the dramatic impact on retirement savings over a 10-year period when companies add a Cash Balance Plan to the existing 401(k) Profit Sharing plan.

Pension Protection Act of 2006 Allows Larger Tax Deductions

Along with law firms and medical practices, many other professional services firms and small businesses are benefiting from higher Cash Balance contribution limits allowed under the Pension Protection Act (PPA) of 2006.

A seven-partner California accounting firm added a Cash Balance Plan several years ago, but their contributions were limited by the pension laws in place at the time. The firm was contributing about $350,000 for the seven partners.

As a result of the 2006 PPA changes, Kravitz redesigned the plan and the seven partners are now enjoying contributions totaling $725,000—more than $100,000 per partner in the Cash Balance Plan alone.

While employees enjoy an enhanced 401(k) Profit Sharing benefit package because of the Cash Balance Plan, this redesigned plan did not cost the firm anything in additional contributions for the staff. The employees were already getting an employer contribution of about 8% of pay.

One of the largest engineering firms in Los Angeles needed to provide a program for additional tax-deferral for dozens of its partners. The 401(k) Profit Sharing contributions of $49,000 were just not enough. In 2006 Kravitz designed a Cash Balance Plan and the firm will contribute $7,000,000 into the plan, with many of the partners receiving their age-weighted maximum in the plan. The guaranteed interest crediting rate (ICR) for this plan is about 5% which excited many of the partners who saw large losses in their 401(k) Profit Sharing accounts in 2000 and again in 2008.

The new Cash Balance Plan was a win for the partners and a win for the employees, who also received enhanced retirement benefits.

What this Means for Financial Advisors

Think about the case studies we've reviewed here and look for similar prospects who have delayed retirement savings and need advanced strategies for company retirement plans. Medical groups, professional services firms, family businesses, and closely-held businesses with several owners are often excellent candidates.

When you meet highly compensated individuals who are frustrated by the contribution limits on their 401(k) and Profit Sharing plans, you'll be ready to offer them an innovative solution. You may want to share with your clients these five solid reasons for considering a Cash Balance Plan:

Top Five Advantages of Cash Balance Plans

1. **Reducing taxes**

   Funds contributed to Cash Balance Plans are tax-deductible, and the earnings grow tax-deferred until the money is withdrawn. This benefit is enormous and can have a dramatic impact on savings accumulation. At retirement or when leaving employment, a Cash Balance account can be rolled into an IRA and no taxes are due until age 70½, at which point only a very small portion of the money is taxed.

2. **Accelerating retirement savings**

   Business owners and partners can often more than double their annual pre-tax retirement savings when a Cash Balance Plan is added to a 401(k) Profit Sharing plan. Many find they can squeeze 20 years of retirement savings into 10.

3. **Attracting and retaining top talent**

   Like all qualified plans, Cash Balance Plans require contributions to non-owner employees, a requirement that becomes a key benefit for many firms. Money that would otherwise have gone to the IRS is now enriching both the employer's and employees' retirement savings, helping to attract, reward and retain talented employees. Professional services firms find Cash Balance Plans a great incentive on both the partner and employee level.

4. **Shelter from creditors**

   Assets in a Cash Balance Plan are protected from creditors in the event of a bankruptcy or lawsuit. In volatile economic times, preserving profits from both taxes and creditors is increasingly important.

(continued on next page)

(continued from previous page)

5. **Protecting retirement savings from market volatility**
   Because investments are usually tied to a conservative benchmark such as the 30-year Treasury rate, Cash Balance Plans have avoided the dramatic fluctuations seen in 401(k) accounts over the past few years. While 401(k) account holders often rely on higher risk strategies to maximize growth, Cash Balance Plans grow primarily through high contribution amounts earning interest rates that stay ahead of inflation without taking on major risk.

What's Next for Financial Advisors?

Now that you've reviewed some case studies and you understand how Cash Balance Plans enhance the 401(k), it's time to look more specifically at the competitive advantages for business owners. Adding a Cash Balance Plan can make a tremendous difference in a firm's ability to attract and retain top talent. Chapter 4 offers case studies on the recruitment power of enhanced corporate retirement packages, and lists three key questions to ask before adding a Cash Balance Plan.

3

Winning the War for Talent: How Cash Balance Plans Change the Game

From the board room bunkers to the cubicle trenches, competition to find and retain top talent is becoming tougher than ever. Leading global consulting firm McKinsey & Company recently updated their notable 1998 study, *The War for Talent*, concluding that the most important corporate resource for the next 20 years will be talent. More important than capital or technology, talent is also the resource in shortest supply. In our highly competitive global economy, the best people are willing to change jobs often, and attrition rates are climbing in many organizations.

Now more than ever, the quality of company-sponsored retirement plans plays a crucial role in attracting and retaining first-rate talent. For many high income professionals, retirement plans are one of the most important sources of wealth accumulation. And for some companies, retirement plans can be the single greatest source of tax benefits. Consequently, any organization that wants to win the war for talent must have a highly competitive retirement package.

So what makes a retirement plan compelling to talented, in-demand professionals? A generous 401(k) Profit Sharing plan is a good start. Add a Cash Balance Plan, and the attraction is significantly greater. In fact, adding a Cash Balance Plan to an existing retirement package is often the most cost-effective way to create a winning retirement package.

The Retention Power of a Cash Balance Plan

Let's illustrate the concept by looking again at the world of law firms. With a Cash Balance Plan in place, law firm partners are able to have more of their pre-tax income deferred to retirement accounts. Recent tax law changes and plan design options allow tax-deductible Cash Balance Plan contributions from $35,000 to over $200,000 annually, depending on participants' ages. Law firms making these Cash Balance contributions have greatly improved partner satisfaction with retirement plans.

Most retention efforts focus on the first few years of employment. Losing an attorney after a long recruiting effort can be demoralizing and expensive.

While it's expensive to lose talented attorneys early in their careers, it's even more devastating to lose them mid-career. Mid-career lawyers are often in their prime in terms of productivity, skill and client retention. Their loss can greatly affect the firm's quality of work in addition to its bottom line.

A law firm's retirement plan can be a crucial factor in an attorney's decision to leave. Attorneys in their 40s have often paid down student loans and gotten their mortgages in check. Looking ahead at their financial futures, they typically feel behind in retirement savings. Attorneys, like physicians, start later than many professionals in saving for retirement due to student loans and years of lower paid work as associates. If the firm doesn't help them meet their financial objectives, they will probably find another firm that can.

The single most important step a law firm, medical group, or any competitive organization can take to improve its retirement plan is to increase pre-tax contributions so partners can grow their qualified retirement accounts. This can be accomplished by adding a Cash Balance Plan to the retirement plan already in place—typically a 401(k) Profit Sharing Plan. By adding Cash Balance, contribution amounts can double or even triple for partners in their 40s and 50s.

The Limited Recruitment Value of 401(k) Plans

Before looking more closely at the competitive features of Cash Balance Plans, we need to step back and review why winning companies don't limit themselves to 401(k) plans. It's true that 401(k)s remain the fastest growing type of retirement plan in the US, but they pose serious challenges in terms of low contribution limits and the investment risk borne by plan participants. It helps to know that 401(k)s were never intended to replace the traditional defined benefit pension plans that once dominated in corporate America.

As costs for employee medical benefits skyrocketed in the 1980s and 1990s, many business owners had to cut costs on the pension side. Many moved away from costlier, traditional defined benefit pension plans toward 401(k) plans which were less expensive to operate and allowed greater flexibility for employer contribution levels. This shift also removed the investment risk for employers.

Unfortunately, the explosion in 401(k) plans has had serious consequences: more and more people are retiring without enough funds to support their standard of living. Typically, the problem is that they did not (or could not) defer enough income. A second issue is that 401(k) accounts heavily invested in equities suffered devastating market losses in the recent bear markets of 2000 and 2008. Tens of thousands of Americans saw 50% or more of their 401(k) savings wiped out.

For 2010, the maximum annual 401(k) plan contribution is either $16,500, or for those 50 or older, $22,000. A Profit Sharing plan can provide another $32,500 per year of employer contributions. Unfortunately, once the $49,000 or $54,500 maximum annual contribution has been reached, these plans are maxed out for the year. For professionals and business owners who had to delay retirement savings until mid-career, it's almost impossible to catch up on building healthy retirement portfolios given the limits of defined contribution plans.

Why Winners Need a Higher Octane Qualified Plan

Facing the limits of a 401(k) Profit Sharing plan, some business owners and high income professionals turn to savings and investment vehicles outside of a qualified plan, such as insurance products and after-tax retirement accounts. However, that means missing out on the enormous financial benefits of a tax-favored qualified plan.

The following graph is an illustration of the difference in an account balance over time between saving $50,000 pre-tax in a qualified plan and paying the tax on $50,000 and saving the difference.

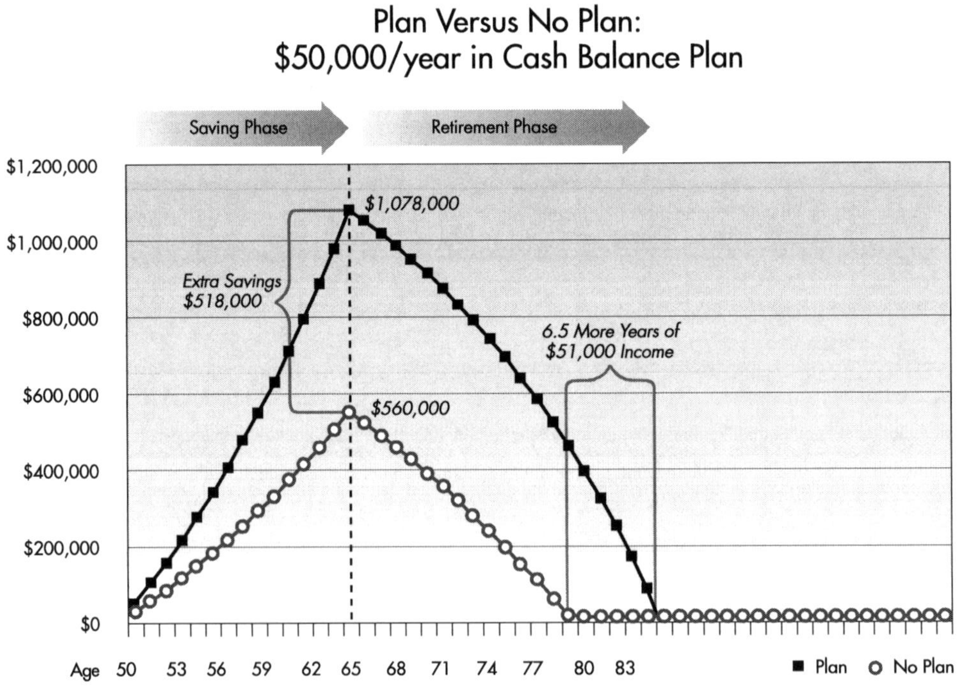

Plan Versus No Plan:
$50,000/year in Cash Balance Plan

Assumptions: Tax rates the same both phases (45%); interest earned in plan: 5%; interest outside plan: 6%; long/short term capital gains rate average: 33%

Adding a Cash Balance Plan (or a defined benefit plan) is the only way to increase contributions within a qualified plan after reaching the limits of a 401(k) Profit Sharing plan. As our case studies have shown, business owners can increase contributions substantially—up to $200,000 per year of deferred taxable income depending on age.

The chart below makes it easy to see just how much of an impact adding a Cash Balance Plan can make. The difference in tax-deferred savings is huge, and increases significantly based on age. Considering how many talented mid-career professionals urgently need to accelerate their retirement savings, it's easy to see the recruiting power of a Cash Balance Plan. And when it comes to retaining key partners and staff, the allure of Cash Balance is just as significant.

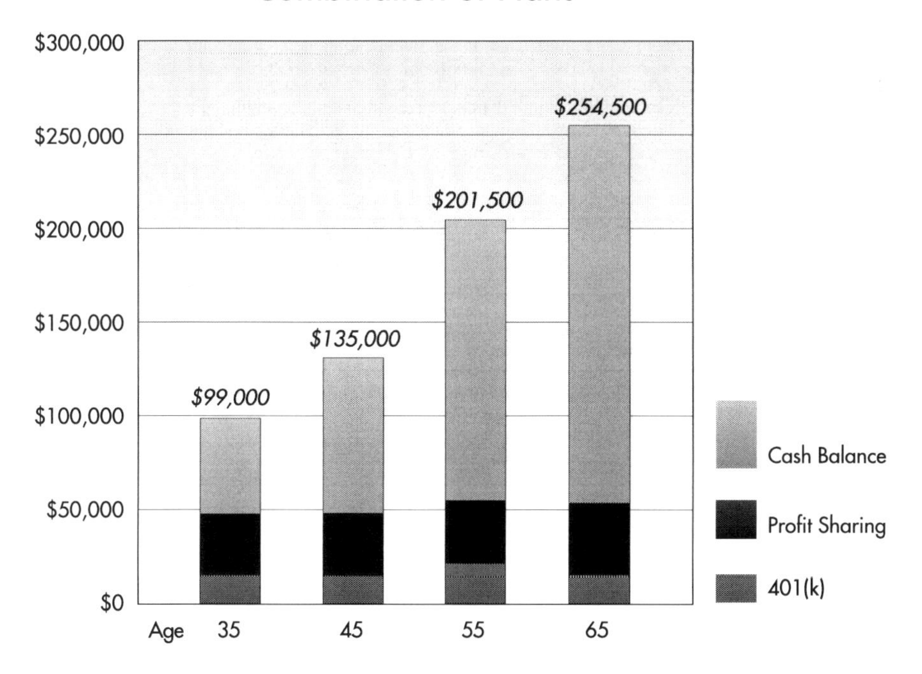

Watching Your Money Grow: the Appeal of Participant Statements

Cash Balance Plans offer many advantages over traditional defined benefit plans. One of the most appealing is that each participant has an individual account and can track its growth on an annual participant statement. Each owner or employee also knows exactly how much is being contributed on his or her behalf, what the interest crediting rate is, and what the final benefit will be. However, because plan assets are pooled and invested collectively, these accounts are "hypothetical" and the plan participant bears no investment risk.

Cash Balance participant accounts are maintained by the third party administrator (TPA), who generates annual participant statements like the one shown below:

Sample Participant Statement
Period of 1/1/2010 through 12/31/2010

John Doe
4944 Lombardy Drive
Los Angeles, CA 90605

Beginning account balance $143,549.00

2010 employer contribution ....$ 70,000.00

2010 interest credit $6,502.77

Ending account balance $220,051.77

Vested percent on 12/31/10 ....100%

Vested balance on 12/31/10 ....$ 220,051.77

Security and Stability: the Comfort of a Guaranteed Interest Credit

After the wild market ride of 2008, owners and employees alike are looking for security, longing for reassurance that their retirement savings can grow safely and steadily. This is yet another key recruitment and retention feature of Cash Balance Plans: the annual interest credit is guaranteed and is not dependent on the plan's investment performance. Furthermore, the nature of a Cash Balance Plan dictates that plan assets be invested conservatively—typically in diversified fixed-income portfolios.

Most Cash Balance Plans are tied to a conservative benchmark similar to the 30-year Treasury rate, which has hovered around 5% in recent years. All accounts are invested collectively by the Plan Trustee in one pooled account, taking away the risk factor of individual account holders choosing their own investments. We'll review all of these investment issues in more detail in Chapter 4.

Case Study: a Small Business Owner Wins the War for Talent

As a small business owner, what would you do if the government offered to pay retirement benefits to your employees? And give you all the credit? And pay you for letting them do it?

This is exactly what the government is doing for many small business owners who set up qualified plans like a Cash Balance Plan. Let's look at an example to see just how valuable this tax incentive can be.

Richard Rozanski is a 40-year-old entrepreneur with a small but profitable furniture manufacturing firm in Florida. Last year, Richard's company contributed $50,000 to a Cash Balance Plan. Of the total, $40,000 went into Richard's account and the remaining $10,000 was divided among the accounts of his four employees as a tax-deferred benefit. The money went into a trust fund where it will grow tax-free until it is paid out as retirement benefits. Richard's company gets a tax deduction for the full $50,000.

Fast-forward 25 years. Richard is now 65 years old and his own account is worth $2.5 million, assuming he has continued making contributions every year and the plan assets earned an annual average of 5%. The employees watched their accounts grow to $500,000 over the years. Without a doubt, the Cash Balance Plan helped Richard attract and retain many talented staff members.

Without the company retirement plan, Richard may have paid himself most of the $50,000 as additional salary, which would be taxable income. If he had invested the extra cash, he would have paid taxes each year on the investment income. At the end of 25 years, at a marginal tax rate of 40%, he would have $1,125,000—less than half the amount he'd have in his Cash Balance Plan retirement account.

Richard does have to pay taxes when he withdraws his money from the plan. At the 40% tax bracket, even if he took it all out and paid all of the taxes at age 65 he would net $1,500,000, about 33% more than he would have without a retirement plan. These numbers get even better if he continues to defer paying taxes until he needs the money to live on or until the government requires it starting at age 70½.

So, by adding a Cash Balance Plan, at the end of 25 years, Richard has more money, his employees have more money, and his employees give him all the credit!

Three Questions to Ask Before Adding a Cash Balance Plan

Plan design is the due diligence phase of adding a plan to a company's overall retirement program. Work with your actuarial partner to consider the following issues for appropriate plan design:

1. **Which subgroups within the organization will benefit from the plan?** Using the medical group example, the group may include shareholder doctors, other physicians, mid-level providers including nurse

practitioners and various levels of administrative staff. Depending on compensation level and the goals of the group, not all subgroups need to be included in the plan. Some firms exclude or 'carve out' groups that receive other types of benefits, such as sales staff who earn commissions.

2. **What employer contribution levels are necessary to ensure compliance with IRS nondiscrimination testing?**
   All retirement plans that enjoy tax-qualified status must pass nondiscrimination testing. These tests are designed to prevent the skewing of benefits in favor of highly compensated employees (those earning $110,000 or higher in 2010). These tests are complex, but they essentially compare rates of deferral and benefits between the "highly compensated" and the "non-highly compensated." Most plans must be tested annually.

3. **Does a Cash Balance Plan make sense for our organization?**
   Due to the complexity of Cash Balance Plans, they involve higher administration fees than 401(k) plans. The decision to adopt a Cash Balance Plan should include a careful analysis of the organization's current and future benefit objectives.

Cash Balance Plans have important legal compliance and actuarial certification requirements. It can be costly and painful to work with an inexperienced provider who is unfamiliar with these issues. Advisors and their clients should seek counsel from an actuarial firm with proven Cash Balance Plan experience, a firm familiar with the intricacies of companies such as theirs. Partnership with trusted experts is the best way to ensure cost-effective long term success for your retirement plans.

Quick Summary of Cash Balance Plan Benefits:

- ✓ *Allows* higher contribution amounts.
- ✓ *Accelerates* retirement savings.
- ✓ *Combines* nicely with 401(k) and/or Profit Sharing Plans for even higher contribution amounts.
- ✓ *Easy to understand and communicate benefits* since participants have individual accounts.
- ✓ Growth of retirement benefit is *not* dependent on investment earnings.
- ✓ *Portable* in the event of job-change or termination.
- ✓ Assets are *protected* from creditors in the event of bankruptcy or lawsuits.

What's Next for Financial Advisors?

What happens to your client's money once it's invested in a Cash Balance Plan? Financial advisors and their clients are not expected to understand all the nuances of the actuarial science behind hybrid retirement plans. However, it's prudent to understand the key investment principles for Cash Balance Plans in order to make informed decisions. Selecting an appropriate investment strategy is critical to the long-term success of the plan. The next chapter explains the investment side of the equation.

4

The Investment Side of the Equation

Warning: before you proceed into this chapter, you need to put aside what you've learned from the defined contribution investment world. The investment strategy for a Cash Balance Pension Plan is very different from the strategy for a 401(k) plan, a Profit Sharing plan or even a traditional defined benefit plan. Applying traditional defined contribution or defined benefit investment principles to Cash Balance Plan assets could spell disaster for your client.

A Unique Investment Objective

Let's start at the beginning. In a 401(k) plan, the investment risk is borne by plan participants. Participants structure their portfolios based upon risk tolerance, investment objectives, and investment horizon. When they retire or leave the company, they get to withdraw their contributions plus or minus their investment earnings.

The protocol is different in a Cash Balance Plan. While the 401(k) plan participant seeks to *maximize* the return, the Cash Balance Plan sponsor seeks to *optimize* the return. As an advisor, you'll need to be familiar with seven fundamental principles that should drive your Cash Balance Plan investment strategy.

Seven Fundamental Investment Principles for Cash Balance Plans

Principle #1: Preserving the Tax Deduction is the Primary Goal

Remember that the primary motivation for establishing most Cash Balance Plans is to reduce taxes and accelerate retirement savings in a tax-deferred account. Since there are consequences for how the investment strategy performs (see Principle #7), it is imperative that the strategy remain consistently in alignment with the primary objective. An investment strategy that reaches for additional return will be out of synch with this objective, regardless of how it actually performs.

Principle #2: Investments are Pooled, Not Self-Directed

Cash Balance Plan contributions are invested by the plan's trustees in a pooled arrangement. There can be no individual account management of plan assets, and IRS regulations do not permit self-direction. This can be confusing, since one of the advantages of a Cash Balance Plan over a traditional defined benefit plan is that participants have individual account balances. Each participant does receive an annual statement showing his or her account balance, contributions and interest credit; however, these accounts are hypothetical. All assets are in fact pooled.

Principle #3: The Plan Sponsor Bears the Investment Risk

Since plan assets are pooled, investment performance risk lies entirely with the plan sponsor rather than the participants. Whether returns are positive or negative in any one year makes little difference to the rank and file participants in a Cash Balance Plan, since they are guaranteed the interest credit stated in the plan document. This is in direct contrast to 401(k) plans, where each participant bears the risk associated with investment selection and performance.

In our view, this is one of the key advantages of Cash Balance Plans for non-partner participants. Investments are handled for them and a positive annual return is guaranteed. It's also a significant benefit for those with large account balances in the Cash Balance Plan, since it keeps a certain percentage of their overall wealth conservatively invested through all market cycles. This security can allow them to be more aggressive with their personal investments or 401(k) Profit Sharing plan holdings, since a portion of their assets is always shielded from the next market bubble.

Principle #4: The Plan Must Guarantee an Annual Interest Credit

All Cash Balance Plans have at least two things in common. Every plan has a guaranteed annual interest crediting rate (ICR) written into the plan document, and every plan is required to meet that ICR each year. This ICR drives the plan's funding and benefits. It can be a fixed rate or a variable rate linked to an index, in accordance with IRS guidelines.

There are a number of options for choosing a plan's ICR, discussed in more detail in the Appendix at the end of this book. The ICR used by a majority of plan sponsors is the 30-year Treasury bond yield, as listed in section 417(e) of the Internal Revenue Code. Averaging 5.88% since 1977, it's a target rate that strikes the right balance between the actuarial and investment issues surrounding interest rate selection. The investment strategy must be structured to "hug" the targeted ICR each and every year, otherwise plan sponsors face consequences for overperforming or underperforming, discussed in Principle #7.

While nearly all Cash Balance Plans in existence today use a yield-based structure for the ICR, a small minority use a return-based structure. See the Appendix for a more in-depth discussion about ICR structures.

Principle #5: The Interest Crediting Rate Cannot Exceed a Market Rate of Return

IRS guidelines state that an ICR cannot exceed a "market rate of return." The interesting thing about this mandate is that the IRS has yet to clearly define it. In the Cash Balance world, we know what would *not* qualify as an acceptable ICR, such as anything based on equity returns. However, that leaves a great deal of room for interpretation as actuaries and their clients attempt to strike the right balance between the various investment and actuarial issues.

IRS Notice 96-7 has provided some safe harbors for what the IRS would consider an acceptable ICR, such as the yield on the 30-year Treasury rate. The long anticipated IRS regulations, set to come out late in 2010, will add clarity to this issue.

Principle # 6: Plan Assets Must be "Marked to Market" at Year-End

Another big difference between Cash Balance Plans and their 401(k) Profit Sharing counterparts is the investment horizon. Defined contribution plan participants have the luxury of riding out market cycles waiting as long as it takes for the markets to recover. Cash Balance Plans do not have that luxury. In effect, Cash Balance Plans have a one-year investment horizon. The ICR stated in the plan document must be achieved each year, or there are consequences. Thus, a strategy structured for any other time frame—which is virtually every investment strategy using a "relative return" style of investment management—is flawed from the start.

Strategies structured for longer time horizons are bound to get caught in the wrong investment cycle, which could decimate plan assets, as seen in the 2008 market sell-off. The Appendix discusses two additional investment time horizons at play within Cash Balance Plans.

Principle #7: Overperforming or Underperforming the Interest Crediting Rate (ICR) Results in Serious Consequences

Toward the end of each year, Cash Balance Plan investments are reviewed and the plan actuary certifies the funding status of the plan. If the investments have outperformed the ICR, the excess return must be both recognized and realized the following year. That means reduced contribution amounts and smaller tax deductions for owners, which can defeat the purpose of having a Cash Balance Plan.

If the plan has underperformed the ICR, plan sponsors must make an additional contribution to maintain the plan's "fully funded" status. If the plan sponsor doesn't make up the shortfall by the company tax filing deadline, the IRS considers it underfunded, and the sponsor faces a series of restrictions. Although losses can be amortized over seven years, plan assets may be frozen and distributions may be restricted. The consequences for over- and underperforming are discussed in the next section of this chapter, and in further detail in the Appendix.

Risks of Overperforming or Underperforming

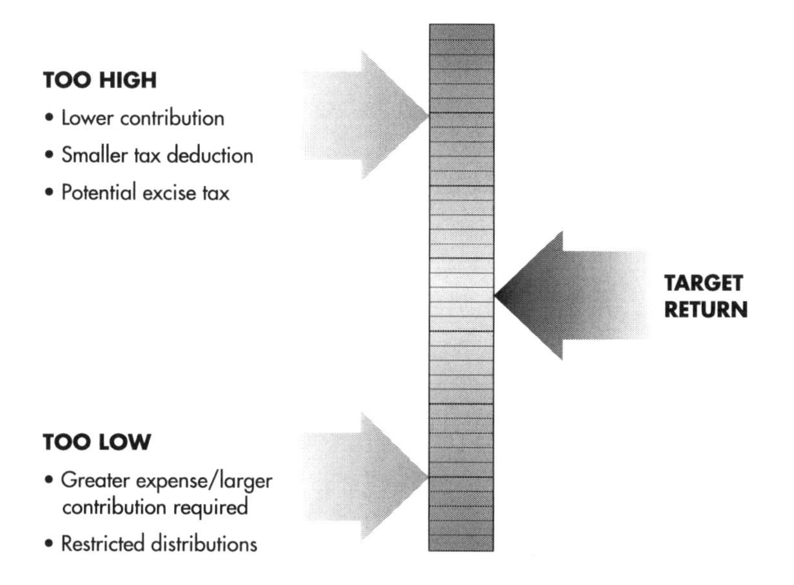

What Happens When You Apply Traditional Investment Strategies to a Cash Balance Plan?

In two words, potential disaster. The past decade produced many cautionary tales for Cash Balance Plan investment advisors. Captured by dreams of soaring returns during a prolonged bull market, many plan sponsors and their advisors threw caution to the wind and made the mistake of treating the Cash Balance investment strategy the same as a 401(k) Profit Sharing plan. Defined contribution plans can tolerate losses, even dramatic ones, since plan participants have the luxury to wait out bear markets and benefit from an eventual recovery with no additional contributions required.

During the bull market of 2003 through October 2007, some Cash Balance Plan investment advisors were loathe to structure conservative portfolios with benchmarks like the 30-year Treasury yield. Striving for 4% to 6% when they were witnessing significant returns in stock funds, particularly sector funds such as emerging market and energy funds, presented a psychological hurdle. As a result, some Cash Balance investment strategies were structured with equity allocations of 30% to 80%.

Most of these plans faced serious consequences and penalties in the bear market of 2008. Clients whose investment advisors ignored our advice saw their plan assets reduced by as much as 50%, and many company owners were forced to dip into cash reserves to make up the losses.

We know of one plan sponsor, a law firm, whose $2 million Cash Balance Plan lost 20% of its value in 2008. In order to remain fully funded, the firm had to make up a $400,000 shortfall, plus the required interest crediting rate of 5% ($100,000) plus the actual required contribution amount for that year. The firm's typical contribution of $150,000 per partner soared to $275,000 per partner in order to keep the plan fully funded.

IRS Restrictions on Underfunded Cash Balance Plans

Funding Target Attainment %	Effect on Distributions
100% or Higher	Plan is Fully Funded, No Restrictions
80 - 99%	Sufficient Funding, Some Restrictions on Officers/Owners
60 - 79%	Plan "At Risk," Lump Sums Are Restricted for All
Below 60%	Plan is "Distressed," No New Benefits or Lump Sums

Many companies faced these dramatically higher contribution requirements at a time when the economy was in a deep recession, profits had plummeted and cash flow was restricted.

While Cash Balance Plan losses can be amortized over a seven-year period, failure to keep the plan fully funded can result in benefit restrictions, payout restrictions to highly compensated employees, quarterly funding requirements and participant notifications, among other challenges. The chart above provides a summary of IRS restrictions on underfunded plans. The underfunding issue becomes even more complex and challenging if one or more of the participating partners leaves the firm and is no longer available to help cover the losses.

The Ideal Solution: A Customized Cash Balance Investment Strategy

By now you understand the critical importance of an investment strategy designed specifically for Cash Balance Plans. A conservative absolute return-based strategy that specifically targets the interest crediting rate benchmark each year, while limiting volatility and mitigating losses, is an ideal solution for Cash Balance Plan sponsors.

Ideally, the strategy will achieve an investment return, net of all expenses, that "hugs" the ICR. A relative return strategy with a longer investment horizon tied to different benchmarks would be unsuitable for Cash Balance Plans. We discuss this issue in greater depth below.

By hugging the ICR (such as the 30-year Treasury rate) on an annual basis, a conservatively managed, customized Cash Balance investment portfolio can reduce the risk of overperforming or underperforming the ICR. This strategy ensures that the company's tax deduction goals can be consistently planned for and preserved.

Digging Deeper: Why Relative Return Strategies Don't Work for Cash Balance Plans

Performance measurement is a major difference between Cash Balance investment strategies and those employed for defined contribution and traditional defined benefit plans. Defined contribution plans use mutual funds measured by *relative performance:* their performance is compared to a relevant benchmark index or to peer mutual funds within their asset class or style group.

A relative return based performance manager takes the approach of managing a portfolio within a full market cycle, which can range from six to eight years. These managers are not focused on the immediate, annual return. Rather, they concentrate on benchmarks and indices. They take a much longer view, content to find securities trading at discounts to their intrinsic value or growth rate, and hold positions over the long term. For example, at the bottom of the bear market in 2009, some portfolio managers were buying securities such as GE, JP Morgan, Bank of America, Microsoft and others, theorizing that these securities would be much higher in five to 10 years.

Many advisors and plan sponsors have tried a relative return strategy for Cash Balance investments. They may have been intentionally seeking higher risk adjusted returns over the benchmark, or unintentionally using relative return based funds in an asset allocation model trying to hit a target return over a one-year period.

While a relative return based strategy is perfectly acceptable in 401(k) plans or personal investing with long term horizons, it is not appropriate for Cash Balance Plans, which must be marked to market each year. The table below illustrates the poor fit of a relative return strategy. A 60/40 balance account over two decades simply doesn't work for meeting yearly funding requirements.

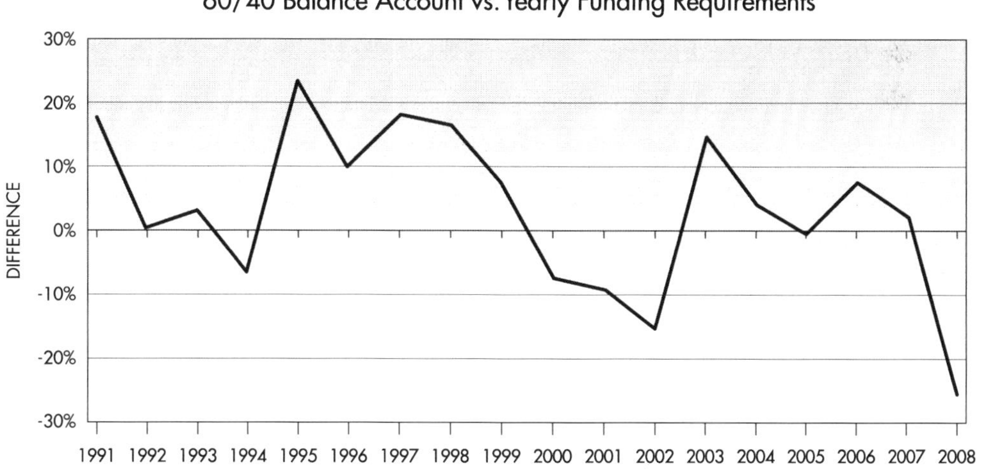

A traditional asset mix may generate the required return over a decade or more, but the yearly volatility is inappropriate for a cash balance plan.

60%, S&P Index, 40%, Lehman Aggregate Bond Index.
Calendar year returns, gross of fees.

A case study brings home this point perfectly. Late in 2008, one of our clients had had enough of the losses suffered in his Cash Balance Plan account and informed his advisor that he wanted to change direction and find a strategy designed specifically for Cash Balance Plans. The stunned advisor said to him, "But I don't understand. I know we're down 13% for the year, but the S&P 500 is down over 20%. We've done a heck of a job!" Clearly, he did not understand the dynamics of a Cash Balance Plan and the required 5% interest crediting rate that the client's plan guaranteed to all participants that year. Enter the absolute return strategy.

Absolute Return Strategies: the Key to Success for Cash Balance Plan Investments

An absolute return strategy targets a specific investment return, and then structures the investment strategy to meet that objective in the appropriate time frame, regardless of market conditions, while managing risk exposure.

The only important benchmark is the targeted rate of return, which the investment manager has broad latitude to achieve. The absolute return portfolio manager takes the view that there's always a bull market somewhere, and makes it his job to find it—or just enough of it to hit the plan's targeted return.

The absolute return based fund manager avoids the strange incentives generated by traditional benchmarks used in relative return strategies, such as "defining risk as active risk instead of total risk, and an inducement to buy last year's winners with new money coming into the fund."[2]

An absolute return strategy that specifically targets the interest crediting return benchmark each year, while limiting volatility and mitigating losses is exactly the strategy needed for a Cash Balance Plan. Many traditional mutual fund strategies are inappropriate for Cash

---

[2] Ineichen, Alexander M. *Absolute Returns: The Risk and Opportunities of Hedge Fund Investing* (Wiley, 2002)

Balance Plans. Balanced Funds, Asset Allocation Funds (such as risk-based or date-based investment strategies) or a blend of Equity Index and Fixed Income Strategies have all been used with problematic results. Even though they may have outperformed their relevant benchmarks, they held disastrous results for Cash Balance Plans in 2008. Conversely, during bull markets, these funds often generated excessive returns that reduced the company's planned tax deduction. Even worse, if the plan was terminating, the sponsor faced heavy excise taxes for overfunding.

It's All About the Risk: Achieving Security in Down Markets

On many fronts, 2008 was a revelation. It highlighted the dramatic difference in downside protection between relative and absolute return approaches. Traditional mutual fund strategies based upon relative return provide little protection in down markets. At best, investment managers may raise their cash positions as high as the prospectus will allow them, or for those that allow hedging, might take a short position in stock index futures.

Nearly all money management firms shared the same fate in 2008. Seeing storm clouds on the horizon in 2007, many portfolio managers began raising their cash positions to 20%, a fairly defensive move. Unfortunately, they were bound by other parameters and when the financial storm hit in 2008 and 2009, their funds were badly damaged. They saw it coming, but couldn't get out of the way. They were not alone. Virtually all fund managers whose funds mandated staying invested in equities in any meaningful way were crushed.

This problem is clearly explained in Alexander M. Ineichen's book *Absolute Returns:*

> *"The main reason why traditional funds do poorly in down markets is that they usually have to have a certain weight in equities according to their mandate and therefore are often compared with a car*

> *without brakes. The freedom of operation is limited with traditional money managers...."*

Absolute return managers who have a targeted return level with few constraints are in a much better position to protect Cash Balance Plan clients when they need it most, in a declining market.

The starting point for an absolute return fund manager is the targeted interest crediting rate (ICR) for the year in question. Working from a conservative core blend of cash and fixed income asset classes, the prudent manager will "take what the markets provide" in pursuit of the targeted return.

If the ICR can be attained through the conservative blend of cash and short duration fixed income, then the portfolio will resemble a multi-sector bond fund for that particular year. If additional alpha is needed, the prudent manager will implement conservative trades in different asset classes, with tight stop-losses, to generate the additional return. Positions will be driven, as they should be, by investment opportunities that surface each day, week or month and the fund manager's own dynamic risk/reward evaluation process.

A Cautionary Tale: The Math Behind Cash Balance Plan Losses

It is very important for advisors, plan sponsors and other key decision makers, regardless of their sophistication level, to fully understand the math behind Cash Balance investment losses.

Let's say you had a choice between two investment returns. You could earn 5% every year for 10 years or you could earn 8% every year for five years and then lose 20% for one year and then earn 8% annually for the next four years. Which option would you choose? You might choose the second one because it averages 5.2% over the entire period instead of 5%. However, doing so with a plan required to make $100,000 annual contributions would cause the plan to be almost $40,000 underfunded. So instead of increasing the return for your client, you would actually be decreasing it. And if those numbers don't sound big enough, try it with 6% instead of 8% and the plan now has a $250,000 shortfall. So why would a client want to take on all of that risk just for an extra 1% return? It just isn't worth it.

Clearly, the risk of outperforming the interest credit rate on a Cash Balance Plan is just not worth it. As simple as it sounds, the trick is not to lose money. The key to investing Cash Balance Plan assets is to have steady returns every year.

An Investment Strategy That Beats Inflation 9 Out of 10 Times

One investment question you may hear from Cash Balance prospects is this, "So I'm more protected in a down market, but at what cost? Am I protected against rising inflation?"

Some clients may wonder whether an investment strategy that focuses on long term Treasury yields is an effective approach for outperforming inflation. In addition to hitting the plan's interest crediting rate, beating inflation remains a top priority.

As you can see in the following chart, long term Treasury yields have consistently outperformed inflation over the last 60 years. From 1952 through December 31, 2009, long term Treasury yields outperformed headline inflation over 90% of the time.

The conclusion is quite persuasive. Not only does the investment strategy minimize volatility in the portfolio and keep the asset trajectory on the right course, but it also outperforms inflation on a consistent basis.

Long Term Treasury Yields vs. Headline Inflation

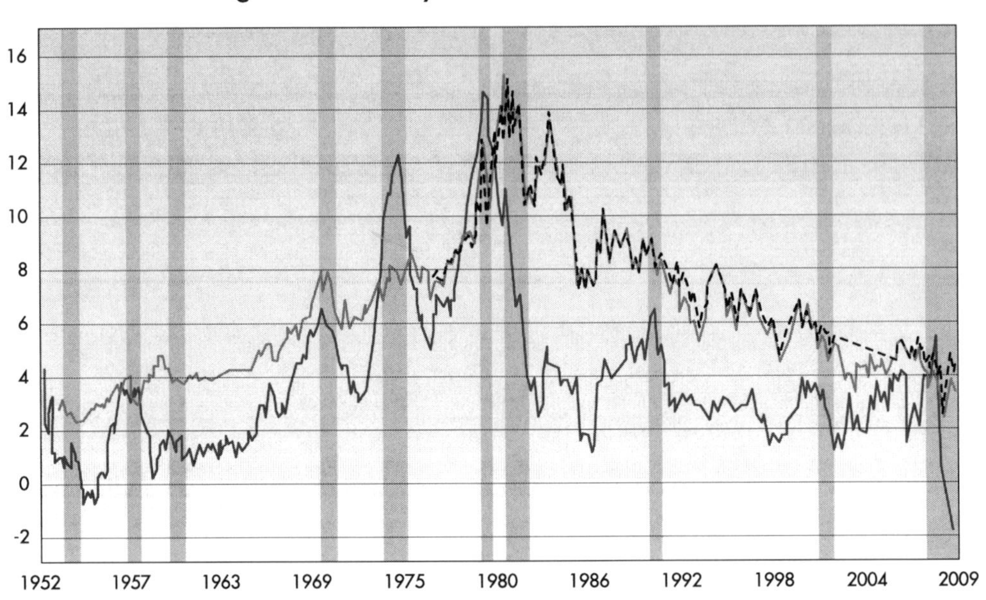

— (% 1-Year) CRI-U All Items U.S. City Average SA 1982-84=100 – United States

— Constant Maturity Yields 10-Year, USD, Yield, Percent, Average – United States

-- Nominal Yield on U.S. Treasury Bonds with Constant Maturity, 30-Year, Nsa – United States

▪ Recession Periods – United States

Finally, a Word About Investment Fees

In the defined contribution world, investment management fees are a critical component of the long term success of the investment strategy. As we go to press, there is growing regulation, legislation and litigation over fees charged in retirement plans. This pressure is designed to hold plan fiduciaries accountable to determine whether the fees charged to plan participants are reasonable in light of the services being rendered.

While this may sound counterintuitive, there is no equivalent fiduciary pressure in the Cash Balance environment. That's because plan participants are provided with an interest credit each year that is guaranteed by the plan sponsor. It is not about actual investment performance here; it's about predictable, consistent investment performance. None of the potential fees associated with a Cash Balance Plan—investment management, product/contract asset charges or advisor compensation—impact the plan participants.

While fees are an important consideration in the overall picture for Cash Balance Plans, it is important to understand, and equally important to educate plan sponsors, that fees are secondary to the success of the strategy itself. In 2008, dozens of low-cost fixed income, equity and asset allocation funds from very reputable fund families were decimated by market volatility. And the Cash Balance Plans that were utilizing them were punished as well.

The return, net of all fees, is the crucial factor in a Cash Balance Plan. If the fee structure consistently prevents the strategy from attaining the investment objective, then fees need to be re-evaluated. However, if the investment goal is consistently achieved within the established fee structure, the actual dollar amounts should be less of an issue.

Let's put the fee issue into perspective: in the fall of 2008, an advisor we were working with decided against a customized Cash Balance investment solution and instead chose a well-known index fund family's conservative low cost alternative, using a relative return style of management. The plan adopted the low-cost strategy and then lost nearly 10% in Q4 2008. As this example illustrates, the critical issue is not the fees—it's about stable returns, net of fees.

What's Next for Financial Advisors?

If you've started to wonder why Cash Balance Plans aren't more popular and more widely known, you'll find some answers in our next chapter, *Myth Busting 101*. For many years, legal questions persisted, and there were controversies over converting older defined-benefit plans to Cash Balance Plans. Myths and misconceptions from this era still persist. We'll arm you with the true facts about Cash Balance Plans so you can clear away misunderstandings when it comes time to sell.

5

Myth Busting 101: the Truth About Cash Balance Plans

Why aren't Cash Balance Plans more common, given the powerful financial benefits they deliver to business owners and employees? Why are they still the best kept secret in the pension industry?

We hear these questions frequently from advisors in our Cash Balance Coach® training program. One obvious answer is that there are a lot of myths and misconceptions about Cash Balance Plans floating around. Unfortunately, this "myth-information" prevents thousands of business owners from taking advantage of the single most significant retirement savings and tax-deferral opportunity available.

Some of these myths are based on out-of-date information. Others arose from an era when major national corporations were converting large defined benefit plans to hybrid plans, creating legal challenges unrelated to the Cash Balance Plan model we use today.

This chapter will empower you with myth-busting facts so you can counteract objections and answer clients' questions truthfully and intelligently.

Myth #1: Cash Balance Plans violate the law

The Truth: The 2006 Pension Protection Act (PPA) gave Cash Balance Plans a legal green light and removed uncertainty about their status.

Prior to the PPA, there were a number of court cases and congressional hearings associated with Cash Balance Plans (primarily large plans converting from defined benefit to hybrid), with lawyers arguing that the conversion discriminated against older workers. This issue was clearly resolved by Congress in 2006, and properly designed plans consistently receive favorable IRS determination letters.

It also helps to remember that the IRS has approved thousands of Cash Balance Plans since the first one was introduced in 1985. If the government believed these plans were not beneficial to employees, they would certainly have taken steps to stop their implementation long ago.

The PPA not only removed remaining uncertainty about Cash Balance Plans, it increased allowable contribution levels. The only major legislative efforts currently underway that may impact Cash Balance Plans are designed to ease funding requirements, allowing underfunded plans more time to recover from the economic downturn.

Today, if a Cash Balance Plan is in trouble with the IRS, it's an issue of poor plan design or major funding shortfalls. The best way to prevent problems like these is to partner with experts, including an experienced pension actuarial firm that successfully manages a variety of Cash Balance Plans.

Myth #2: Cash Balance Plans are inflexible

The Truth: With creative plan design and careful planning, Cash Balance Plans offer flexibility and a wide range of options.

Like other myths about Cash Balance Plans, this one arose from safe harbor traditional defined benefit plan designs. As hybrids, Cash Balance Plans combine the portability of defined contribution plans with the high contribution limits and stability of a defined benefit plan. Think of them as the best of both worlds.

In the design phase of a Cash Balance Plan, business partners can decide the exact plan formula to achieve their desired contribution levels. They can also choose to exclude some employees or partners if they desire, as long as the plan passes all required nondiscrimination tests. The plan can be used to equalize contributions between owners of different ages. Owners also can use the plan to reward certain groups of employees, balancing out other types of compensation and benefits.

Cash Balance Plans are highly flexible when combined with 401(k) Profit Sharing plans, offering a variety of "mix and match" plan design options. An experienced pension actuarial firm with Cash Balance expertise can show you a range of creative plan design options to meet your clients' goals.

Myth #3: You have to make a 10-year commitment to have a Cash Balance Plan

The Truth: There is no 10-year commitment required, and plans can be frozen or terminated if necessary.

While some employers have a Cash Balance Plan in place for 10 years or longer, others keep these plans for a shorter time period. For example, advisors sometimes suggest a Cash Balance Plan as a strategy for family business succession planning, when older owners need to build retirement savings rapidly and turn the business over to the next generation.

If a company can commit to maintaining the chosen contribution levels (as set out in the plan document) for at least three years, a Cash Balance Plan makes sense. The plan document can be amended to change contribution levels, though this must be done before any employee works 1,000 hours in a plan year. In cases of company financial difficulties, a plan can be temporarily frozen, or terminated.

Myth #4: Cash Balance Plans are risky

The Truth: Major risks associated with traditional defined benefit plans are gone from Cash Balance Plans.

Different calculation formulas determine the lump sum payouts of Cash Balance Plans, mitigating many of the risks of runaway costs in a traditional defined benefit plan. Cash flow risks can be minimized with good plan design, and employers can reduce contributions to themselves in a slow business year, as long as it's done before they have worked 1,000 hours.

The first risk that disappears with Cash Balance Plans is the risk of higher salaries determining the benefit near retirement age. Most traditional defined benefit plans use a formula that uses a percentage of highest final average compensation multiplied by years of service; it becomes as if the participant earned his or her highest compensation every year. It's possible to use a career average pay formula in a traditional defined benefit plan, but that can make it more difficult to get the owners a maximum contribution.

The second risk in a traditional defined benefit plan is the risk of hiring or retaining older employees. In a Cash Balance Plan the formula can be designed as a percentage of pay or a flat dollar amount, neither of which are dependent directly on age. In a traditional defined benefit plan the lump sum is always dependent directly on age since the benefit is defined at Normal Retirement Age instead of as the sum of hypothetical allocations and interest. Older employees cost more in a defined benefit plan than they need to in a Cash Balance Plan.

The third and most important risk is the interest rate risk. This one is the hardest to understand, but it is the biggest reason most companies are abandoning their traditional defined benefit plans in favor of Cash Balance Plans. Both types of plans have interest rate risk, but the severity is much different. In a Cash Balance Plan, the risk is not earning the guaranteed rate. In a defined benefit plan, the risk is not only not earning the guaranteed rate, but also the liabilities changing in value.

Let's look at an example since this is a difficult concept to grasp. Let's say that as of January 1, 2010 a traditional defined benefit plan and a Cash Balance Plan with the same demographics both have $1 million in assets and liabilities. Both plans would be perfectly funded if terminated immediately. Let's also say that the interest rate for valuing liabilities is 5% for 2010, 6% for 2011 and 4% for 2012, and nothing else changes during those three years. Finally, we'll assume that both plans earn 5% on assets each year.

Both plans will have assets and liabilities of $1.05 million at the end of 2010, but on the first day of 2011 the defined benefit plan liabilities will change overnight to be roughly $0.87 million. This leaves the plan in an overfunded status and will reduce the 2011 contribution. The Cash Balance Plan still has assets and liabilities of $1.05 million.

At the end of 2011 both plans have assets of about $1.10 million. The defined benefit plan has liabilities of $0.92 million and the Cash Balance Plan has liabilities of $1.11 million. At the start of 2012 the interest rate has now dropped to 4%. The Cash Balance Plan is still $0.01 million underfunded whereas the defined benefit plan now has liabilities of about $1.25 million and is $0.15 million underfunded. That difference requires a higher contribution and all of the problems we discussed in Chapter 4 that go along with underfunded plans.

The key point demonstrated by our example is that Cash Balance Plans are relatively predictable while traditional defined benefit plans are unpredictable. Their costs depend heavily on interest rates that fluctuate from year to year. No asset manager can predict how interest rates will change from year to year, and even if they could, they couldn't achieve the returns necessary to keep the contributions from fluctuating. When interest rates go up, the plan would have to lose money to avoid being underfunded, and when interest rates went down the fund would have to have huge returns. Doesn't that seem backward?

News stories about underfunded defined benefit plans almost always date from periods of low interest rates. This is due to the inverse relationship between interest rates and liabilities, and the only way to get rid of that risk is to adopt a Cash Balance Plan instead of a traditional defined benefit plan.

Myth #5: Cash Balance Plans discriminate against older workers

The Truth: Congress, court rulings, and the 2006 Pension Protection Act have all clearly stated that Cash Balance Plans do not violate age discrimination laws.

In 2004, the US House of Representatives Committee on Education and Labor held a hearing called, "Examining Cash Balance Pension Plans: Separating Myth from Fact." Much of the testimony given attested to the fact that when Cash Balance Plans are set up properly, they do not violate age discrimination policies. Committee chairman Rep. John Boehner of Ohio said:

> *"Most courts have ruled no age discrimination occurs with Cash Balance Plans if the pay and interest credits given to older employee accounts are equal to or greater than those of younger employees. The most recent ruling on this topic, issued just last month in the Tootle case, agrees that Cash Balance Plans are not inherently age discriminatory."*

In fact, age discrimination is far more likely in traditional retirement plans. Benefit values in a final average pay defined benefit plan are heavily skewed in favor of older employees. In contrast, Cash Balance Plans provide benefit values much more evenly over an employee's career.

It may seem that younger employees receive greater benefits under Cash Balance Plans than older employees, but this is not true. Although the younger employees have longer compounding of interest credits, these really can be seen as adjustments over time, in the same way that inflation is adjusted. As long as all employees participating in the Cash Balance Plan receive the same interest crediting rate regardless of age, there is no age discrimination.

What about when a company converts a traditional defined benefit plan to a Cash Balance Plan? That means shifting from a plan that already disproportionately favors older employees to one that is relatively age-neutral. The change may reduce the expected benefits of older workers, but it does not take away anything they were entitled to in the old system. Because the outlook for pension growth changes under the new plan, many employers will voluntarily adjust the plan to cushion this change for employees at or near retirement age.

Myth #6: Cash Balance Plans only benefit highly compensated employees

The Truth: Cash Balance Plans are required by law to pass nondiscrimation testing, and many non-partner employees benefit significantly. Cash Balance Plans typically serve to attract and retain staff at all levels, not just the highly compensated.

While Cash Balance Plans offer business owners significant tax breaks and high contribution limits for themselves, the plans are required to deliver meaningful benefits to all participants. In fact, a 2010 report by Kravitz showed that rank-and-file employees realize a 100% increase in company contributions if their employer adopts a Cash Balance Plan. Contributions to non-partner employees are usually in the range of 5% to 8% of pay, often in combination with contributions through an existing Profit Sharing plan.

The flexibility and portability of Cash Balance Plans is also a great benefit for rank-and-file employees who are unlikely to stay with one employer for decades. The unique design of Cash Balance Plans make them beneficial to other groups of employees as well, specifically women and younger workers.

Women sometimes find it more difficult than men to build retirement security, since they're more likely to take time out of the workforce to care for children or elderly family members. Women also change jobs more frequently than men, spending an average of 4.8 years with each employer. With interrupted earnings records, women can lose the opportunity to vest and have fewer years in which to contribute to retirement plans.

Nancy M. Pfotenhauer, President of the Independent Women's Forum, spoke about this issue before the House Committee on Education and Labor during the 2004 Congressional hearings on Cash Balance Plans. She said:

> *"In the opinion of the Independent Women's Forum, traditional retirement and pension approaches simply fail to meet the needs of our changing society. These modernized pension arrangements have evolved to suit today's more mobile workforce and respond to employee preferences for transparency, portability and the accrual of more meaningful benefits earlier in a career.*
>
> *"As you know, unlike traditional defined benefit plans where a significant portion of the benefits go to the relatively few workers with very long service, benefits in so-called hybrid plans grow more evenly over a worker's career and are distributed more equitably across short-, medium-, and long-service workers. For the vast majority of employees who no longer spend a full career with one employer, a hybrid plan will produce higher benefit levels than a traditional benefit plan at equal cost."*

One benchmark study done in 1998 by the Society of Actuaries found that 77% of women do better under a Cash Balance Plan than a traditional defined benefit plan. They are better off because they move in and out of the workforce in order to balance family needs, and because they cannot afford to take early retirement.[3]

The same study found that two-thirds of all employees included would have received higher benefits under a Cash Balance Plan than a traditional defined benefit plan.

The nature of business has changed. Younger workers prize job mobility and change jobs more often than those in previous generations. Cash Balance Plans allow a potential employer to be competitive in attracting employees by offering flexible retirement savings that allow for earning benefits earlier in their careers.

Myth #7: Cash Balance Plans are confusing and hard for employees to understand

The Truth: Cash Balance Plans are simple for participants to understand and the benefit from the employer is transparent. Only the actuarial math is complicated.

With clear, simple participant statements, a fixed annual employer contribution (either a flat amount or a percentage of pay), and a guaranteed annual interest credit, Cash Balance Plans offer highly appealing transparency.

Employees can easily see how much their employers are contributing, how much interest their accounts are earning, and how much they'll receive when they leave the company or retire.

While 401(k) plans still play a vital role, employees recovering from bear market losses especially appreciate the security of a Cash Balance

[3] Kopp and Scher. Society of Actuaries. "A Benefit Value Comparison of a Cash Balance Plan with a Traditional Average Pay Defined Benefit Plan." October, 1998.

Plan with its guaranteed interest credit and conservative investment approach.

Some people may imagine that employees prefer older traditional defined benefit plans because they're used to them. However, very few employees understand how they earn benefits in a traditional defined benefit plan, or what those benefits would be worth if they left before retirement. This confusion is one reason why employers look to Cash Balance Plans. When an employee can see a beginning-of-year and end-of-year dollar value balance, it's easy to appreciate how much the employer is contributing on his or her behalf.

Myth #8: Cash Balance Plans are expensive to set up and maintain

The Truth: Weigh the annual tax savings against the plan administration costs, and it's much more expensive not to have a Cash Balance Plan.

This myth falls under the category we call "The High Cost of a Cheap Retirement Plan." Because Cash Balance Plans must be maintained by an actuary and have more complex compliance testing requirements, their administration costs are roughly double that of a 401(k). But there's simply no comparison with a 401(k) when it comes to contribution levels and tax savings—the Cash Balance Plan often delivers more than double the financial payoff.

Some people also have the misconception that small businesses can't afford Cash Balance Plans. In fact, owners of companies with fewer than 50 employees often enjoy proportionally greater rewards from a Cash Balance Plan than owners of larger companies. It becomes a simple math equation to compare the administrative costs and contributions to employees with the company's overall tax savings.

What's Next for Financial Advisors?

Now that you understand the many advantages of Cash Balance Plans and you're armed with facts for myth-busting, it's time to delve into plan design. Chapter 6 will help you understand all the variables that go into creating an effective plan design that will meet a business owner's needs while passing nondiscrimination testing.

6

Compliance, Complexities and the Importance of Smart Plan Design

By now you're aware that Cash Balance Plans are not "off the shelf" retirement solutions. While these plans deliver tremendous benefits, they involve many variables and are essentially custom designed for each client's needs.

Your role as an advisor is to help your client negotiate the many choices involved in establishing a Cash Balance Plan. You will also need to help your client choose an experienced pension actuary who can design a plan that fulfills those goals while passing all required IRS compliance testing.

This chapter will help you understand compliance tests and how a Cash Balance Plan can be thoughtfully designed to pass them. We also discuss how the PBGC affects contribution levels, and other topics related to funding and accrual of benefits.

While you don't need to understand these issues in detail, it is very helpful to have a solid grasp of the underlying concepts when you introduce Cash Balance Plans to prospects. Just as importantly, you need to be aware of what you don't know, and where to turn for help when clients pose questions you can't answer.

What are Nondiscrimination Tests?

The Internal Revenue Code prohibits qualified (tax-favored) retirement plans from disproportionately benefiting highly compensated employees over non-highly compensated employees. A retirement plan must pass IRS nondiscrimination testing annually, proving that the plan continues to be fair to all participants. There are a variety of ways to prove non-discrimination; fairness can be based on either contributions made or retirement benefits received. An experienced actuarial firm will work closely with you and your clients to design a plan that passes annual testing while meeting business objectives.

How can you tell if a Cash Balance Plan for a prospect will likely pass testing? If the company already has a New Comparability 401(k) Profit Sharing Plan in place, adding a well designed Cash Balance Plan will usually pass, since it will be tested in combination with the existing plan.

New Comparability: How Cross-testing Demonstrates Nondiscrimination

A New Comparability Profit Sharing plan divides employees into groups in which each receive an employer contribution at a different percentage of pay. The plan does not require an equal percentage of pay because it compares benefits at retirement age, rather than present contribution amounts. New Comparability plans generally work best if the owner is at least 10 years older than some of the employees.

Since older employees have fewer years for their retirement plan contributions to grow with interest, higher employer contributions allow them to make up the difference. In the following table, you can see that although contributions to the older and younger employees are unequal percentages of pay, by retirement age, they will have comparable benefits.

When a company has a Cash Balance Plan, more significant employer contributions are going to the highly compensated employees (usually older business owners) than to other employees. In order to pass testing,

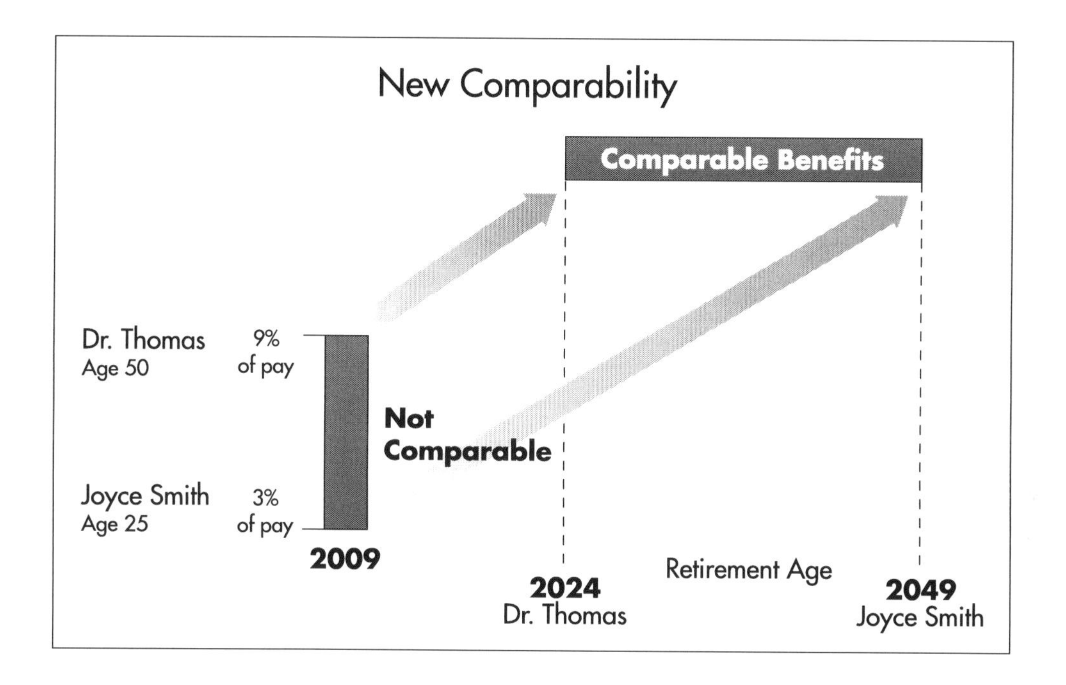

the Cash Balance Plan is usually combined with a Profit Sharing plan and the two plans are tested together. Since Profit Sharing Plans generally make larger contributions to employees than do Cash Balance Plans, it helps balance the overall contributions in order to satisfy nondiscrimination testing.

Gateway Testing

Gateway testing is used to demonstrate nondiscrimination in Profit Sharing plans by establishing a minimum percentage-of-pay contribution for non-highly compensated employees. The minimum is generally set at 5% to 7.5% of pay when a Profit Sharing Plan is combined with a Cash Balance Plan to pass testing. However, in certain circumstances, in order to pass other tests, a higher percentage may be required.

Keep this feature in mind when looking for prospective Cash Balance clients. If a company is already making 5% of pay contributions to employees in a Profit Sharing plan, it may be a strong Cash Balance candidate.

Minimum Participation Requirement

The minimum participation requirement, defined under Internal Revenue Code 401(a)(26), is another safeguard to prevent discrimination. Does that mean everyone in the company needs to be included in a Cash Balance Plan? Not at all, in fact, participation levels are very flexible when the plan is first set up. As we discussed above, Cash Balance Plans are typically tested together with a 401(k) Profit Sharing Plan, so not everyone needs to receive a Cash Balance contribution in addition to a Profit Sharing contribution. For IRS purposes, a participant is someone who is receiving a "meaningful benefit" from the plan; the options for establishing this meaningful benefit are described in detail in the section below.

If there are only two potential participants, both must participate. But in a company with three or more potential participants, the minimum participation level is the lesser of 1 and 2 below:

1. At least 40% of eligible employees (i.e. 8 out of 20 employees = 40%).
2. 50 total employees.

For example, a firm with 200 eligible employees can meet IRS participation requirements by including just 50 people, rather than including 40%, or 80 employees. This feature is one of the many flexible aspects of Cash Balance Plans.

There are a number of plan design techniques to satisfy minimum participation requirements. As a financial advisor, you'll work with your client to effectively define the company's goals and then work with an actuarial firm who can design a plan to fulfill those needs.

In this next example, there are eight potential participants. By the 40% calculation, only four must participate in the plan. Only the Doctor, Spouse, and two employees need to be included in the Cash Balance Plan. Of course, the employees who are not part of the Cash Balance still receive a Profit Sharing contribution from the employer.

Minimum Participation – Example 1

Name	Age	Annual Salary	401(k)	Profit Sharing	Cash Balance	Total Contribution
2 Owners						
Doctor	63	$245,000	$22,000	$14,865	$0 to $200,000	$236,865
Spouse	55	$50,000	$22,000	$0	$0 to $5,000	$27,000
Subtotals		**$295,000**	**$44,000**	**$14,865**	**$205,000**	**$263,865**
6 Staff				*5.5% of pay*		
Employee 1	60	$38,000		$2,090	$0	$2,090
Employee 2	45	$35,000		$1,925	$0	$1,925
Employee 3	36	$35,000		$1,925	$0	$1,925
Employee 4	31	$31,000		$1,705	$0	$1,705
Employee 5	30	$27,000		$1,485	$500	$1,985
Employee 6	24	$23,000		$1,265	$500	$1,765
Subtotals		**$189,000**	**$0**	**$10,395**	**$1,000**	**$11,395**
Grand Totals		**$484,000**	**$44,000**	**$25,260**	**$206,000**	**$275,260**
					Percent to Owners:	**95.9%**

In our second example, 53 shareholders have chosen to participate in the Cash Balance Plan, satisfying the minimum participation requirement. Therefore, there is no need to include the non-owner employees. Nondiscrimination in this case is established with a 6% Profit Sharing contribution to employees.

Minimum Participation - Example 2

Compensation	401(k)	Profit Sharing	Cash Balance	Total Contribution
53 Shareholders				
$245,000	$16,500	$32,500	$55,000 *(Average)*	**$104,000**
68 Shareholders				
$245,000	$16,500	$32,500	$0	**$49,000**
240 Employees				
varied		*(6% of pay)*	$0	*(6% of pay)*

Meaningful Benefit Testing

Proving that a Cash Balance Plan delivers meaningful benefits to participants is part of the compliance testing process; however, the IRS allows plan sponsors various options in this regard. The government defines "meaningful benefit" as an amount equivalent to an annual benefit of 0.5% of pay, paid as a lifetime annuity at retirement age. Since this calculation of meaningful benefit is based on age and compensation, it would be different for each employee. Other options can be used instead, establishing consistent contribution levels that are simpler to explain.

While it's possible to have employees participate in a Cash Balance Plan at a level below the "meaningful" amount, they will not count toward meeting the minimum participation requirements we described above.

Option 1: Meaningful Benefit Amount

In this option, each participating employee's contribution amount is based on the actuarial calculation of a meaningful benefit. This can be a higher cost option, but the formula used to calculate the benefit allows it to remain in place for a number of years with limited amendments, thereby reducing administrative fees.

Option 2: Percentage of Pay

This technique is usually the first one used by clients when establishing a Cash Balance Plan because it is easy to understand. A certain percentage of pay is established to pass meaningful benefit testing. Advantages of this method include ease of planning for contributions, and simplicity in explaining the plan to employees. Also, there is generally no need for plan amendments when participants receive raises, since a percent-of-pay contribution increases automatically.

Option 3: Flat Dollar Amount

This method establishes a flat dollar amount that is applied across all eligible employees. It requires initial calculations to determine a flat amount that will pass meaningful benefits testing. As with percentage of pay, this method means that contributions can be easily planned for and easily explained to employees. However, one disadvantage is that it may need to be recalculated in future years as employee compensation changes and company demographics shift. This is often, though not always, the lowest cost option for employers.

The table below shows how a company could use these three different options for setting Cash Balance employer contributions to pass Meaningful Benefit Testing: (1) "Meaningful Benefit" based on actuarial calculations of a 0.5% of pay lifetime annuity, (2) percentage-of-pay option—in this case, the plan will pass testing with 2% of pay per employee, or (3) a flat-dollar calculation of $500 per employee. In this

Meaningful Benefits – Options for Employers

Name	Age	Annual Salary	Cash Balance Contribution		
2 Owners					
Doctor	63	$245,000	$0 to $43,268		
Spouse	55	$50,000	$0 to $58,480		
Subtotals		**$295,000**			
6 Staff			**Option1:** *Meaningful Benefit*	**Option2:** *2% of Pay*	**Option3:** *Flat Dollar*
Employee 1	60	$38,000	$2,311	$760	$500
Employee 2	45	$35,000	$1,100	$700	$500
Employee 3	36	$35,000	$741	$700	$500
Employee 4	31	$31,000	$526	$620	$500
Employee 5	30	$27,000	$439	$540	$500
Employee 6	24	$23,000	$287	$460	$500
Subtotals		**$189,000**	**$5,404**	**$3,780**	**$3,000**

case, the flat dollar amount is the most affordable for the employer, but this is not always true. Remember that this amount may change as employee demographics and other variables change. An experienced actuarial partner can recommend the right solution based on your client's particular needs.

What is the PBGC and How Does it Affect Cash Balance Plans?

The Pension Benefit Guarantee Corporation (PBGC) is an independent federal agency created by the 1974 Employee Retirement Income Security Act (ERISA), with the goal of protecting employees when a distressed private defined benefit pension plan fails and can't meet its liabilities. The PBGC essentially offers a form of insurance for pension plans. Recent examples include the PBGC taking over United Airlines' pension liabilities after the company filed for bankruptcy in 2005.

Sponsors of defined benefit plans, including Cash Balance Plans, must pay an annual premium ($35 per participant as of 2010) to the PBGC in return for greater security and other benefits. If the plan becomes underfunded, the sponsor must pay an additional premium of 0.9% of the underfunded amount.

A few specific plan types are not covered by the PBGC: a plan is exempt if it includes only "substantial owners" of a business, i.e. every participant owns 10% or more of the business. A plan is also PBGC-exempt if the sponsor is a professional service firm with 25 or fewer active participants. A list of exempt professional service firm categories follows.

The PBGC's creation was driven by public pressure following a series corporate pension plan failures that left many workers desperate. Most prominent was the 1963 Studebaker bankruptcy, when more than 4,500 workers lost their pension benefits.

Professional Service Firms Ineligible for PBGC Coverage (If 25 or fewer active participants)

- Physicians
- Dentists
- Chiropractors
- Osteopaths
- Optometrists
- Other licensed practitioners of the healing arts
- Attorneys
- Public accountants
- Public engineers
- Architects and draftsmen
- Actuaries
- Psychologists
- Social or physical scientists

The most important benefit for companies covered by the PBGC is having no deduction limits on their combined Profit Sharing and Cash Balance contributions.

Challenge: In companies *not* covered by the PBGC, combined employer contributions to the Profit Sharing plan and Cash Balance Plan are limited to 31% of total eligible pay. For example, if the total eligible payroll is $1 million, then employer contribution to both plans together cannot exceed $310,000 (31% of $1 million).

Possible Solution: Maximize 401(k) contributions but limit employer Profit Sharing plan contributions to 6% of total eligible payroll. This technique permits us to maximize the Cash Balance contribution without being subject to the combined plan deduction limits.

Understanding Funding and Allocation Issues

In a Cash Balance Plan, benefits do not have to accrue to participants until they have worked 1,000 hours in a given plan year. For most full-time employees, this falls in the month of June. After the 1,000 hour mark is passed, the annual allocation becomes a legal obligation for the plan sponsor. However, the funds do not need to be deposited until the company tax filing date, or (with extensions) as late as September 15th of the following year for a calendar-year plan.

As an advisor, it is important to address potential issues regarding timing of required allocations with your clients so they can be prepared. When working with multi-partner firms, you'll likely hear questions and concerns about obligations to partners leaving the firm.

If a partner leaves prior to working 1,000 hours and accruing his benefits, he may still feel entitled to his share. To deal with this situation, a firm can make the exiting partner whole by paying him for the months of benefits he had accrued (i.e., 3/12 of the year's total).

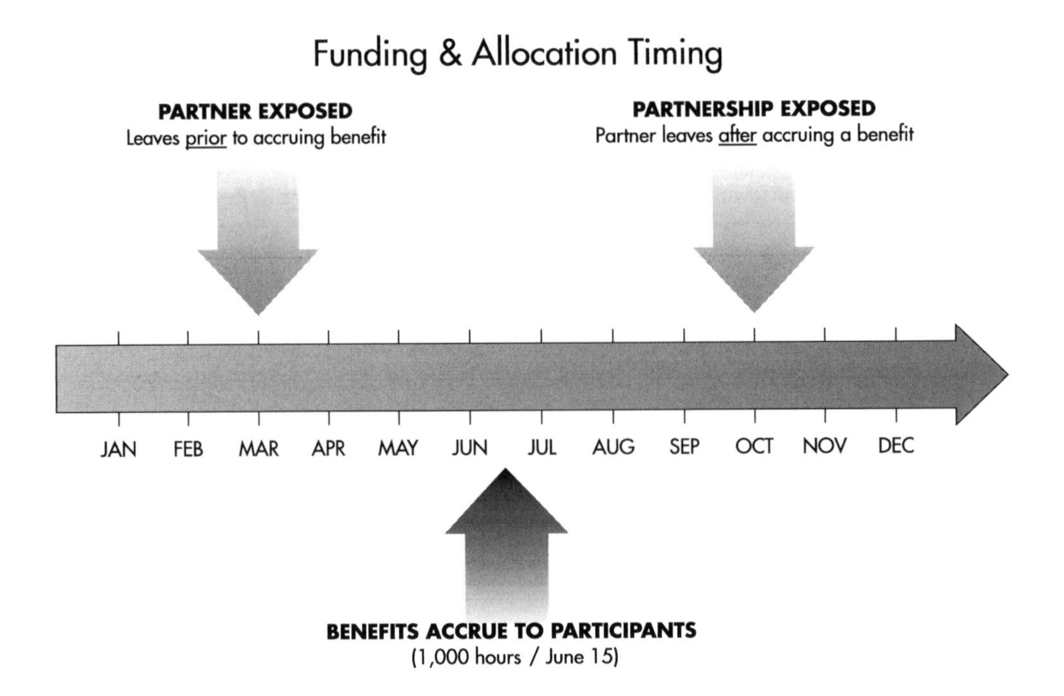

If a partner leaves after accruing the Cash Balance benefit, but before the end of the plan year, the funds can be paid on a "current" basis. That is, the exiting partner's benefits are funded as he earned them (i.e., 10/12 of the year total).

Provisions for these types of partnership issues can be written into the plan document and made clear to all partners who choose to participate in the plan.

It is also important to educate your clients about funding requirements and deadlines. While there is some flexibility for when funds are deposited, underfunding carries serious penalties and can result in distributions being severely restricted or frozen. Funding requirements changed substantially following the 2006 Pension Protection Act (PPA). All Cash Balance Plans must now have their funding status certified by an actuary annually, and may be required to make quarterly contributions if funding drops below 100%.

Again, it is very important to work with an experienced actuarial firm to ensure consistent compliance with the IRS' stringent new funding requirements.

What's Next for Financial Advisors?

An understanding of Cash Balance Plans helps financial advisors grow their 401(k) businesses, opening doors to meeting high net worth professionals and successful entrepreneurs. True, a Cash Balance Plan may not be the right solution for every new prospect or client. But your ability to introduce the Cash Balance option and talk about it intelligently will distinguish you from other advisors, and may bring in new retirement planning business anyway.

How can you identify prospects that might benefit from a Cash Balance Plan? And how do you demonstrate your expertise? The next chapter will teach you how to market your services to clients and grow your retirement business.

7

How to Win the Marketing Battle, from the HR Trenches to the Boardroom Bunkers

In the preceding chapters, you learned about the challenges and complexities of Cash Balance Plans, as well as the many benefits they can bring to your clients. As an advisor who actually understands Cash Balance Plans, you already have a leg up on your competition. But how can you market these services to clients and more importantly, close the deal?

This chapter will teach you various techniques for marketing Cash Balance Plans to new clients. We'll show you how to open doors to areas of business you may not have considered, and we'll give you tips on closing the sale.

The good news is that the market for Cash Balance Plans is growing exponentially. The 2010 Kravitz National Cash Balance Research Report, showed a 359% increase in Cash Balance Plans between 2001 and 2007. In 2001 there were only 1,227 Cash Balance Plans nationwide, and by 2007 there were 4,797. Data from the most recent IRS Form 5500 filings is not yet available as we go to press, but all key indicators suggest that growth will accelerate.

The 2006 Pension Protection Act not only clarified IRS approval of Cash Balance Plans, it raised allowable contribution levels and made the plans easier to implement and operate. These changes, coupled with rising tax rates, the need to recover from market losses, and ongoing market volatility created a "perfect storm" for Cash Balance Plans to soar in popularity.

Financial advisors armed with knowledge from this book are uniquely positioned to take advantage the this growth wave, particularly since almost all Cash Balance Plans are attached to a 401(k) Profit Sharing Plan.

Direct Marketing: Reaching the Right People

The first step in marketing to potential clients is being able to identify ideal candidates for Cash Balance Plans. Databases can be an excellent tool for finding prospects because you can set specific search criteria based on characteristics that make companies a good fit for Cash Balance Plans.

A number of databases take advantage of detailed company retirement plan information that becomes public record when companies file their annual form 5500s with the Department of Labor. Larkspur *(www.larkspurdata.com)* and FreeERISA *(www.freeerisa.com)* are two examples.

From what you've learned in this book, you can choose search parameters to generate lists of targeted businesses most likely to benefit from a Cash Balance Plan.

Sample Database Sorts:

1. Company is currently contributing 3% to 5% of pay or more to a defined contribution plan.
2. Use business codes to target specific industries, i.e. 541110 for law firms or 621111 for medical groups.
3. Geographical area, using zip codes where certain types of businesses are concentrated (a high tech corridor, specialty medical groups clustered around hospitals, etc.).
4. Sort by size of plan assets and employee participation levels to find companies with strong retirement programs in place.

By searching for specific characteristics, you can narrow down prospects from thousands to a small group of highly qualified prospects in your area. The database provides you with the names and phone numbers of executive directors and/or decision makers and marketing efforts should be directed toward them.

If you can get a copy of the prospect's census and/or 401(k) Profit Sharing plan testing reports, then the following are good indicators that they are a strong Cash Balance Candidate:

1. One or more highly compensated employees or key employees are at the 401(k) profit sharing maximum ($49,000 in 2010).
2. At least 10% of the employees are key employees (owners and executives) and are at the maximum compensation limit ($245,000 in 2010).
3. Company is currently contributing 3% to 5% of pay or more to employees.
4. The owners and executives are, on average, older than the non-highly compensated employees.

Get Their Attention

Now that you have a list of prospects, how can you get their attention? Some of the top advisors we work with have used these angles effectively.

Money Talks: The Tax-Savings Opener

One financial advisor opens emails to prospective clients with this simple sentence:

> "Due to changes in the tax and pension laws, there is a new retirement plan available that saves my clients on average nearly $1 million in income taxes."

This should pique the interest of any successful business owner, prompting them to ask you for more information. After a discussion to learn more about the prospect's retirement needs and goals, ask your actuarial partner to run a Cash Balance illustration. You'll be able to demonstrate the specific benefits of Cash Balance for the prospect's company—right down to estimated annual tax savings.

Sample Illustration

Name	Age	Annual Salary	401(k)	Profit Sharing	Cash Balance	Total Contribution	Tax Savings*
5 Partners							
Partner 1	60	$245,000	$22,000	$32,500	$0 to $193,000	$247,500	$99,000
Partner 2	55	$245,000	$22,000	$32,500	$0 to $148,000	202,500	$81,000
Partner 3	50	$245,000	$16,500	$32,500	$0 to $113,000	162,000	$64,800
Partner 4	45	$200,000	$16,500	$28,000	$0 to $75,000	119,500	$47,800
Partner 5	40	$180,000	$16,500	$25,200	$0 to $60,000	101,700	$40,680
Subtotals		**$1,115,000**	**$93,500**	**$150,700**	**$589,000**	**$833,200**	**$333,280**
21 Staff				*7.5% of pay*			
Employee 1	55	$65,000		$4,875	$1,100	$5,975	
Employee 2	55	$65,000		$4,875	$1,100	$5,975	
Employee 3	55	$65,000		$4,875	$1,100	$5,975	
Employee 4	55	$65,000		$4,875	$1,100	$5,975	
Employee 5	55	$65,000		$4,875	$1,100	$5,975	
Employee 6	45	$45,000		$3,375	$1,100	$4,475	
Employee 7	45	$45,000		$3,375	$1,100	$4,475	
Employee 8	45	$45,000		$3,375	$1,100	$4,475	
Employee 9	45	$45,000		$3,375	$1,100	$4,475	
Employee 10	45	$45,000		$3,375	$1,100	$4,475	
Employee 11	35	$30,000		$2,250	$1,100	$3,350	
Employee 12	35	$30,000		$2,250	$1,100	$3,350	
Employee 13	35	$30,000		$2,250	$1,100	$3,350	
Employee 14	35	$30,000		$2,250	$1,100	$3,350	
Employee 15	35	$30,000		$2,250	$1,100	$3,350	
Employee 16	30	$25,000		$1,875	$1,100	$2,975	
Employee 17	30	$25,000		$1,875	$1,100	$2,975	
Employee 18	30	$25,000		$1,875	$1,100	$2,975	
Employee 19	30	$25,000		$1,875	$1,100	$2,975	
Employee 20	30	$25,000		$1,875	$1,100	$2,975	
Employee 21	30	$25,000		$1,875	$1,100	$2,975	
Subtotals		**$850,000**	**$0**	**$63,750**	**$23,100**	**$86,850**	**$34,740**
Grand Totals		**$1,965,000**	**$93,500**	**$214,450**	**$612,100**	**$920,050**	**$368,020**
					Percent of Employer Contribution to Partners:	**89.5%**	

Plan Designs are for illustration purposes ONLY.
**Assuming a 40% tax rate; taxes are deferred only.*

Fear Listens: The Crash Recovery Opener

Many business owners and high income professionals are still reeling in shock from the 2008 market crash and the devastating losses in their retirement portfolios. Some fear that they'll have to postpone retirement in order to rebuild savings, and are desperate for a way to make up their losses.

When contacting potential clients, mention Cash Balance Plans as a means of recovering lost wealth. Since the plans allow older participants to contribute larger amounts, they can make up losses in a much shorter amount of time. This can serve as a powerful marketing tool.

The security and stability of Cash Balance Plan investments is another feature to highlight—we often tell prospects, "Cash Balance is your safe money." If invested correctly (review the guidelines and principles in Chapter 4 of this book), the nature of Cash Balance Plans insulates them from market volatility.

One of our 401(k) clients, a successful Dallas architect, was worried that he would have to work five additional years because of major losses to his 401(k) portfolio and personal investments. He was very pleased to discover that with a Cash Balance Plan, he could accrue up to $2.5 million over the next 10 years and retire when he had originally planned.

The Contribution Limits Table shown on the following page is a very helpful marketing tool, allowing business owners and executives to see exactly how much more pre-tax income can be put away for retirement by adding a Cash Balance Plan.

Contribution Limits

401(k), Profit Sharing & Cash Balance Plans

Age	401(k) with Profit Sharing*	Cash Balance	Total	Tax Savings**
65	$54,500	$200,000	**$254,500**	$101,800
64	$54,500	$205,000	**$259,500**	$103,800
63	$54,500	$209,000	**$263,500**	$105,400
62	$54,500	$214,000	**$268,500**	$107,400
61	$54,500	$203,000	**$257,500**	$103,000
60	$54,500	$193,000	**$247,500**	$99,000
59	$54,500	$182,000	**$236,500**	$94,600
58	$54,500	$173,000	**$227,500**	$91,000
57	$54,500	$164,000	**$218,500**	$87,400
56	$54,500	$155,000	**$209,500**	$83,800
55	$54,500	$148,000	**$202,500**	$81,000
54	$54,500	$139,000	**$193,500**	$77,400
53	$54,500	$132,000	**$186,500**	$74,600
52	$54,500	$125,000	**$179,500**	$71,800
51	$54,500	$119,000	**$173,500**	$69,400
50	$54,500	$113,000	**$167,500**	$67,000
49	$49,000	$107,000	**$156,000**	$62,400
48	$49,000	$101,000	**$150,000**	$60,000
47	$49,000	$96,000	**$145,000**	$58,000
46	$49,000	$91,000	**$140,000**	$56,000
45	$49,000	$87,000	**$136,000**	$54,400
44	$49,000	$81,000	**$130,000**	$52,000
43	$49,000	$77,000	**$126,000**	$50,400
42	$49,000	$73,000	**$122,000**	$48,800
41	$49,000	$69,000	**$118,000**	$47,200
40	$49,000	$67,000	**$116,000**	$46,400
39	$49,000	$62,000	**$111,000**	$44,400
38	$49,000	$59,000	**$108,000**	$43,200
37	$49,000	$56,000	**$105,000**	$42,000
36	$49,000	$53,000	**$102,000**	$40,800
35	$49,000	$51,000	**$100,000**	$40,000

***Assuming 40% tax, taxes are deferred*
**401(k): $16,500; $5,500 catch-up; $32,500 profit sharing*

Drip Marketing vs. Grip Marketing

You may already be familiar with the idea of a drip campaign for marketing professional services. It usually involves sending a series of marketing messages to a large list of prospective clients over a long period of time. The idea is that continuous exposure will make prospects aware of your services, and that they'll eventually call when they need you.

While a drip campaign can be effective for certain services, a Cash Balance Plan is highly specific. If you've used the database sort effectively, you'll have pared down your list to a small group, perhaps 10–30 prospective clients. This calls for a more targeted and concentrated marketing approach, known as a grip campaign.

A grip campaign is designed to get attention quickly. It involves spending a bit more money on a smaller group of prospects. While a potential client may easily throw away brochure after brochure, something tangible and fun will make you memorable.

Here is an example of a grip campaign that we've used with success. You'll find that by the time you're ready to call the prospective client, most will be very amenable to a conversation and will allow you to begin the initial evaluation process that can lead to a sales opportunity.

Grip Campaign: Targeted Direct Marketing

Budget: $950 for 10 recipients

What: Grip campaign in which we send interesting and creative objects to prospects.

Why: To become front of mind with targeted prospects, opening the door for a relationship and sparking interest in Cash Balance Plans.

Who: Ten targeted Cash Balance prospects.

When: Eight week period, with packages sent week one, week four, and week seven. Follow up calls made in week eight.

How: the Breakdown

Week 1 (Estimate: $390)

What:

- $20 Starbucks gift card and mug
- Cash Balance Limits Card and your business card

Where: Starbucks and Kravitz, Inc.

Price: Gift card $20, Mug $12, Cash Balance Plan Limits Card—call Kravitz for free copies

Shipping: $7 each (approximately)

Handwritten Note:

> *"I hope you like Starbucks as much as we do. Enjoy the enclosed Starbucks gift card and mug. I'd love to meet to discuss how we can add value to your company's retirement program. Sincerely, Jim Smith"*

Week 4 (Estimate $260)

What:

- *The Office* Dwight Schrute bobblehead
- Cash Balance Limits Card, Cash Balance article and your business card

Where: NBC.com and Kravitz, Inc.

Price: Dwight Bobbleheads $19

Shipping: $7 each (approximately)

Handwritten Note:

> *"We are unabashed fans of* The Office. *Enjoy. Sincerely, Jim Smith"*

Week 7 (Estimate: $290)

What:

- *The Worst-Case Scenario Survival Handbook: Work* by Joshua Piven and David Borgenicht
- Trail mix
- Heat Treat hand warmers
- Space emergency blanket
- Your business card

Where: Amazon.com, Costco, REI

Price: Book $11, trail mix $5, hand warmers $1.50, blanket $4

Shipping: Free on Amazon.com to the office + $7 each (approximately)

Handwritten Note:

> *"We hope this kit will help you survive the office. We know it can be a jungle out there. I'll be calling your office next week to follow up. Sincerely, Jim Smith"*

Week 8: Call to follow up

- Did you receive the items we sent? Did you enjoy them?
- We also sent some material about Cash Balance Plans.
- What kind of retirement plan do you currently have?
- Are you and your partners happy with the plan?
- Would you and your partners like to save more on taxes and put away more than $49,000 each?
- Can we set up a meeting to review how a Cash Balance Plan might allow you to increase your savings?

How to Get Business Out of Existing Cash Balance Plans

While targeting companies that can obviously benefit from adding a Cash Balance Plan, don't overlook firms with an existing Cash Balance

Plan in place. These plans are still in play, and as a Cash Balance expert you may be in a position to win the business.

While new prospects may need to be convinced of the benefits of a Cash Balance Plan, companies that have one in place are already sold on the idea. Yet there is often a high level of frustration among professional firms over their current Cash Balance situation. Many financial advisors attempting to make Cash Balance Plans part of their business have offered them to clients without being fully aware of the issues at stake. If they partnered with uninformed actuaries who had limited Cash Balance experience, the plan may already be in trouble—not meeting company needs, or running into compliance and funding issues.

Business owners who are struggling with poorly designed, ineffectively managed Cash Balance Plans are prime candidates for a call from an advisor like you, someone who understands the key design issues and investment principles. You have an excellent opportunity to distinguish yourself, guide them in the right direction, introduce them to an experienced actuarial partner, and help get the plan back on track. This approach could lead to the client moving not only the Cash Balance business over to your firm, but the entire retirement program.

Questions to Ask a Prospect With an Existing Cash Balance Plan

- Is the plan design meeting your company's needs and goals?
- Are partners and employees happy with the plan?
- Has the plan continued to pass compliance testing?
- Is the investment strategy meeting your needs?
  - Are contributions consistent or do they fluctuate?
  - Could I view an actuarial report?

Actuaries are required to provide an actuarial report at least once a year that shows contributions, funding levels and how investments have performed. If a prospective client is willing to share this with you, it can give you a clear snapshot of the problems in the plan, allowing you to work with your actuarial partner to suggest solutions.

Focus on a Niche

Focusing your marketing efforts on a well defined niche is another effective strategy for targeting Cash Balance prospects. At Kravitz, our business has focused on law firms and medical groups. By distinguishing ourselves as Cash Balance experts and directing our marketing toward these two groups, we now have almost 200 law firm clients and 200 medical clients.

With a niche focus, you'll become an expert on the particular issues and challenges that affect one profession or industry sector, and you'll immediately impress prospects with your understanding of how a Cash Balance Plan design could meet their needs. A niche focus generates a lot of referrals and word-of-mouth advertising, since many professional communities are tightly knit.

But what niche should you choose? This chart shows the percentage of Cash Balance Plans by business type.

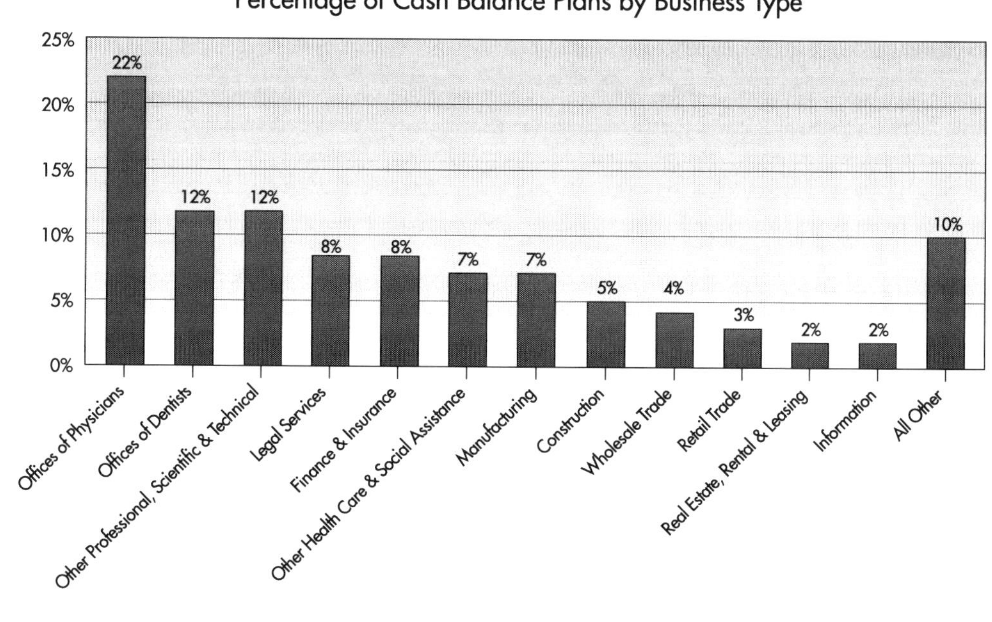

While Cash Balance Plans are currently concentrated in a few industry sectors, do not be too quick to dismiss other business categories. They could present an opportunity for an overlooked niche that you can dominate. For example, small- to mid-sized family businesses in the construction and manufacturing sectors are just discovering Cash Balance Plans, and there is tremendous growth potential. Or think about a "niche within a niche." One wealth manager we partner with has introduced Cash Balance Plans to more than a dozen radiology groups, and he is now firmly positioned as the Cash Balance expert for radiology practices.

Possible Niche Markets

- **Medical groups.** This sector currently has the largest share of Cash Balance Plans. Medical specialists in particular are usually earning enough to need this type of retirement plan. Our clients include diverse specialty practices such as cardiology, neurology, anesthesiology and orthopedics, among others.
- **Law firms.** Legal services firms account for 8% of all Cash Balance Plans and they are well suited to this retirement plan model.
- **Successful businesses in sectors such as engineering, manufacturing, technology, consulting and finance.** Many types of successful businesses are ideal candidates for a Cash Balance Plan. By focusing on a niche that is not as obvious, you could pick up business that other advisors are overlooking.
- **Family businesses.** Family businesses have unique needs and challenges that Cash Balance Plans can address, including ownership structure and succession planning. There's a great opportunity to become an expert on Cash Balance for family businesses.

How do you start building a niche focus? Learn as much as you can about the business issues and challenges facing companies in that sector, through online research, reading professional journals and networking. Reach out to professional and trade association chapters to find out about potential marketing opportunities, such as attending or sponsoring events, or speaking at a luncheon. These organizations are often looking for information on the latest retirement programs.

Position Yourself as an Expert

The key to your marketing efforts will be establishing yourself as a Cash Balance expert. That might be easy to do in a one-on-one meeting with prospects, but how can you demonstrate expertise to a larger audience in your area?

Become Certified as a Cash Balance Consultant

In 2009, Kravitz formalized its educational and marketing support for financial advisors by creating the nation's first Cash Balance Consultant Certification program. Cash Balance Coach® is a four-part webinar series covering all the key elements from plan design to investments and marketing. The program is offered three times annually, or advisors can enroll at anytime in the "on-demand" version for self-paced online learning.

After completing all four webinars, advisors who pass the online exam receive certification as a Cash Balance Consultant (CBC), a designation they may add to their marketing materials or mention in client meetings and presentations. Although Kravitz is not accredited as an educational institution, some advisors have had the CBC designation approved through their firm's compliance process so they can add it to their business cards.

As of summer 2010, more than 400 financial advisors and retirement professionals have completed the Cash Balance Coach® program. CBC alumni continue to network through the Kravitz Cash Balance Consultants LinkedIN group and take advantage of the members-only marketing resources on our website.

Open Doors With An Article

A powerful way to establish yourself as an expert on Cash Balance Plans is to have an article published. Many business and professional publications are interested in articles that clearly explain what can be a rather confusing subject. Now more than ever, professional and industry publications are interested in retirement planning topics, especially articles with new ideas and a fresh perspective.

The article might reach prospective clients in its original run, but more importantly, you can leverage its power by including copies with your marketing materials and mailings to clients. You can feature the article on your website and bring copies to presentations. It's a relatively low-cost investment with a significant return.

Try one of these forums:

- CPA journals and publications
- Local or regional business journals
- Business section of your local newspaper
- Medical, legal and other profession-specific periodicals

Getting published is an important variable in the marketing success quotient. Don't let the excuse that you're not a good writer prevent you from earning a byline. What is essential is your ability to present quality information and ideas. Working with a ghostwriter is an ideal solution, and there are many professional writers eager to find a good assignment. A good place to start is with a professional writers' association in your community. You can conduct an online search, or inquire through a local college's journalism department.

The Kravitz Cash Balance Coach® program also offers a co-authoring option for advisors who want to get published. We connect you with a professional affiliate who is an experienced writer and editor; she helps you select a publication and pitches the article. You can choose to have your article ghost-written or edited. More than a dozen of our Cash Balance Coach® alumni have published articles in professional journals this way, and are using them with great success.

Speaking to Groups

Giving presentations in front of groups of prospects is another excellent way of demonstrating your expertise. You can either host your own event or speak in front of a professional organization.

Option 1: Host an Event. Hosting a "lunch & learn" or a dinner program for a small group of qualified prospects allows you to get in front of potential clients and teach them about Cash Balance Plans. A simple but informative presentation will help them understand the benefits of the plan and why you're the right person to set it up for them. You will, however, be responsible for planning and funding the event.

Ideal Audiences:

- *CPAs.* In the six months after tax season, CPAs have a lighter work load and use this time to educate themselves on developments in their field. The tax savings inherent in Cash Balance Plans make them an important topic for CPAs.
- *Business Owners.* Cash Balance Plans have particular benefits for business owners, but they may feel that they don't know enough to seriously consider it. A presentation and an offer to run a free illustration of the benefits to their specific company will make it simple for them.

We know this works. One of the advisors we work with in Washington state hosts dinner programs for medical professionals. His simple presentation has a high success rate in getting prospects to take the next step and have him run an illustration for their business. After a recent event, he received an email from a neurologist the next morning that said, "Thanks for the dinner last night. Here is the census."

Another advisor in Iowa planned a dinner program for physicians, most of whom canceled or couldn't make it for one reason or another. The silver lining, however, was that just the process of planning and marketing the event led to six appointments with medical directors to discuss whether Cash Balance was right for them.

Option 2: Be a Guest Speaker. Speaking at an event hosted by a local chapter of a business or professional association gets you in front of a large number of prospects without the hassle of event planning. There are a number of professional organizations that regularly host events, as well as more general business groups. Your presentation can be customized to fit any niche group you are targeting.

Ideal Audiences:

- Local business associations.
- Industry-specific organizations with regional chapters.

Your presentation should be simple and informative, demonstrating that you are an expert on Cash Balance Plans. You do not need to get into the complexities, but simply illustrate the benefits that will get the potential client to take the next step.

Our website, *www.CashBalanceDesign.com,* has a member's section for advisors who enroll in our Cash Balance Coach® program that includes helpful marketing and sales tools. One of the tools we offer is a customizable PowerPoint presentation that you can use for speaking in front of groups. Our Coach Program participants can also co-brand tools like our Ideal Candidates Card, which lists top candidates for a Cash Balance Plan along with current plan contribution limits. Marketing materials like these are helpful to distribute at events and often lead to phone calls from prospects.

Make the Sale: Tools to Convert Leads into Clients

Once all your marketing efforts start to pay off, you should be prepared to convert that prospect into a client. The following sales tools and tips can help you make the sale.

On the initial informational call or at your first meeting, we recommend using our Advisor Checklist. Forgetting to ask a key question could lead to problems later in the process. Before we provided the Advisor Checklist as a tool on our website, an advisor was interviewing a potential client and forgot to ask about controlled groups and ownership in other entities. While the business owner seemed like a perfect candidate for a Cash Balance Plan, the question the advisor forgot was crucial. When the ownership in other entities was revealed, the Cash Balance Plan they had designed became very difficult to implement and the advisor lost credibility.

Using this checklist allows you to effectively evaluate whether a Cash Balance Plan is right for your prospect. It also ensures that you have all the critical information gathered in one convenient place for your reference later. You can copy the one we have provided here or make one of your own, but be sure it covers all of these points.

When a prospect contacts you for more information, you should also request an employee census. The census information should include the ages of the owners and the employees participating in the plan, along with estimated annual compensation. This will allow you to work with your actuarial partner to create a Cash Balance illustration.

Once you have an illustration for the company (or a sample illustration if you do not have the census information), you can prepare a short presentation for the executive director or other decision makers. This can be

Cash Balance Plans: An Advisor Checklist

I. Company Structure

A. What business are you are in? ____________________

B. Characterize the entity's profitability/cash flow picture:

1. Steady and consistent, no significant changes anticipated?
2. Volatile swings each year?

C. Ownership structure

1. Number of equity shareholders/owners or partners? _____
2. Number of non-equity partners? _______
3. Number of owners in the following age categories:
   - i. 50 years or older _______
   - ii. 40–49 years old _______
   - iii. 35–39 years old _______
   - iv. Under 35 _______
4. Are tax returns filed consistently by due date? Yes No
5. Controlled Groups
   - i. Does the entity own any other entity? Yes No
     If yes, please provide details ____________________
   - ii. Do any of the owners/partners hold an interest in any other entity? Yes No
     If yes, please provide details ____________________
   - iii. Do any spouses of owners hold an interest in any other entity? Yes No
     If yes, please provide details ____________________
6. Affiliated Service Groups: Does your company work exclusively with any other company or is it affiliated with any other company? Yes No
7. Highly Compensated Employees (HCEs) (>5% ownership or earn in excess of $110,000 per year)
   - i. How many non-owner/partner employees are HCEs? _______
   - ii. What is the attitude of the company/firm toward these HCEs? *(circle one)*
     Include them if possible Exclude them if possible

D. Employee Demographics

1. Generally younger than owners? Yes No
2. Ratio of employees to owners? _______
3. Can you provide us with an Employee Census? Yes No

4. Are there any non-HCEs you seek to benefit? Yes No
   If yes, who? ________________________________
5. Do you anticipate hiring new employees this year? Yes No
   If yes, approximately how many? _______
6. Do you anticipate laying off any employees within the next few years? Yes No
   If yes, approximately how many? _______

II. Current Plan Design

A. Is there an existing 401(k) plan? Yes No
   1. If yes, is it a Safe Harbor plan? Yes No
   2. If yes, is it a match or 3% non-elective? _______
   3. If no, are the owners/key employees restricted in their contributions? Yes No
   4. Do owners/key employees receive refunds? Yes No
   5. What are the eligibility requirements for the plan(s)? _______
   ____

B. Is there an existing Profit Sharing plan? Yes No
   1. If yes, are Employer Contributions consistently made? Yes No
   2. Are the owners able to maximize their contributions each year? Yes No
      i. If yes, what % of owners/partners max out? ______%

C. Are there any other retirement plans in place? Yes No
   If so, what kind?
   [ ] SEP [ ] SIMPLE [ ] Other: ______________

D. What is the name of the TPA firm handling the compliance issues of either the 401(k) or Profit Sharing plan? ______________
   ____

E. List any service/compliance issues that may currently exist in the plan(s)? ________________________________
   ____
   ____

F. Would the owners/partners want to contribute more in tax deferred contributions each year, above and beyond the current limits of the 401(k)/Profit Sharing plan? Yes No
   1. Would their answer to the above question change if they were required to make those same contributions for at least three years before they could change it? Yes No

a PowerPoint or just printed pages, but it must be visual and memorable. The executives you're targeting are extremely busy with a lot of competing demands for their attention. They don't have time to read anything extensive. A chart that shows the immediate benefits to their company in specific terms will be far more effective in starting a discussion.

Your presentation should include the illustration and the current Contribution Limits Chart (shown on page 76). This chart shows the 401(k) and Cash Balance contribution limits for each age group, which illustrates the age-weighting of the plan. The chart also includes a column showing estimated tax savings. Our research indicates that tax savings are the most powerful motivator for adding a Cash Balance Plan. This column shows the dramatic tax deferral possibilities, actual cash savings that the participant will not have to pay the IRS this year.

Working with Actuaries: Why You Need a Strong Partner

After reading the last few chapters, you know that Cash Balance Plans are custom designed for each client and are complicated to set up and administer. Your expertise lies in advising companies on how and why to implement Cash Balance as part of their retirement program, but the design and administration should be handled by a skilled pension actuary with proven Cash Balance experience.

Choosing an actuarial partner should involve due diligence, as with any vendor selection process. Don't make the mistake some advisors and clients have made, choosing an actuary based on price. Poorly (but cheaply) managed plans can run into funding and compliance problems, incurring government penalties and fees. Poorly designed plans are also very unlikely to help your client get the maximum tax deduction. Ultimately, it makes much more sense to invest in getting the plan done right the first time, rather than incurring the high costs of plan termination or takeover by a more experienced actuary.

Six Questions to Ask When Choosing An Actuarial Partner

These five questions will be useful when you evaluate actuarial firms, and can help you make a final decision:

1. **How many Cash Balance Plans do you currently administer?** If the company doesn't handle many plans, they may not have the experience to design and manage your client's plan successfully.

2. **What industries are your Cash Balance clients in?** Plan design issues and challenges vary by industry, so it's best to find a firm that successfully manages Cash Balance Plans in your client's industry. For example, law firms often have multiple tiers of participation and require an understanding of managing partnership risk.

3. **What is the size of the typical plan you handle?** A small firm's Cash Balance Plan is far simpler to manage than one with multiple partners or shareholders.

4. **How many actuaries do you have on staff?** Some firms that administer Cash Balance Plans outsource the actuarial work since they don't have an in-house actuarial team. For reasons of accountability and direct access to expertise, it's preferable to work with a specialized firm whose staff actuaries are highly experienced with Cash Balance Plans.

5. **What do your fees cover?** Ask for a detailed breakdown, and be wary of hidden fees. Also be careful of very low fees and underbidding. Cheap retirement plans become shockingly expensive when they run into compliance and funding problems and need to be terminated or taken over by a more experienced actuary.

6. **Do you have any references I can call regarding your work on Cash Balance Plans?** A good pension actuary will happily provide client references you can call, specifically Cash Balance clients in your industry.

The High Cost of a Cheap Retirement Plan

In many cases, low fees indicate a lower level of service. Remember that the actuary's work reflects on you, and the success of the plan in meeting your client's financial goals depends upon smart, strategic plan design and effective plan administration.

One advisor we now work with managed 10 Cash Balance clients and had in the past chosen an "affordable" actuarial firm to handle administration of all the plans. After a general lack of responsiveness and poor quality of actuarial review, he eventually found out that the firm had little experience with Cash Balance Plans. They had seemed like a great deal at the time—but the pain resulting from the poor work was not worth it. He risked losing not only the Cash Balance Plans, but also his core business of 401(k) plans attached to them.

Sales and Marketing Timeline

Cash Balance Plans can be marketed and sold throughout the year, but in reality most sales happen between September and December. The government deadline for new calendar-year plans is December 31.

Use this timeline as a guide to pace your sales and marketing efforts throughout the year.

January 1–April 15: Prospecting and developing your marketing plan.

April 16–September 1: Executing your marketing plan; building relationships, tax planning with CPAs.

September 2–December 15: Peak selling season; generating plan illustrations, following up with all existing prospects, and closing new business.

New Cash Balance Plan documents must be signed by the client no later than December 31, and since it can take two weeks or more to create and finalize a plan document, most experienced actuarial firms have an early December cut-off date.

The Last Word: Five Tips From Top Advisors

We asked our network of financial advisors around the country to share their tips on making the Cash Balance sale. Here are the five best tips from top producing advisors:

1. **Develop a "champion" and limit the size of your sales audience.**
   In companies with many partners or owners, it can be difficult to sell them all on a Cash Balance Plan at once. Instead, identify a "champion" within the company—the executive you need to convince first, who can then sell it to the rest of the company. Early meetings should probably be limited to a small group and should include the managing partner or executive director who will be able to answer your key questions.

2. **Taxes, taxes, taxes ("Are you looking for a larger deduction?").**
   Today, more than ever before, anxiety about rising tax rates is the key motivating factor for business owners and high income professionals. Tax liabilities are the biggest expense after payroll for many companies, and everyone is looking for a break. The Cash Balance story has never been more compelling, and a simple question like "Are you looking for a larger deduction?" is a great way to open the door.

3. **Involve the firm's tax advisor early, and get him to think it was his idea.**
Nobody likes to be left out, and a CPA is no exception. The last thing you want is to spend time developing a Cash Balance Plan for a company, only to have the CPA put the kibosh on it because he didn't feel he was consulted early enough in the process. The solution is to bring the tax advisor in early and explain the benefits of Cash Balance Plans to him, capitalizing on what knowledge he already has. The tax savings are so significant that with education and supporting materials, a CPA will likely be eager to recommend the plan.

4. **Remind the prospect that "Cash Balance is your safe money."**
This is a good strategy as it emphasizes the conservative nature of Cash Balance Plans and the protection against market volatility. It also opens the door to discussions about the opportunities for meeting clients' long-term objectives, including their after-tax money and profit sharing investments.

5. **Build your business by helping a key center of influence build his business ("You scratch my back, I'll scratch yours.").**
Another strategy is to work with a CPA who is targeting a particular niche, such as legal or medical groups, and help him or her understand Cash Balance Plans and their potential for expanding business. By helping them, they'll be willing to help you in turn. Most top advisors we work with have strong partnerships with a CPA, and there is a constant stream of client referrals going back and forth between the two firms.

What's Next for Financial Advisors?

Our next chapter provides a historical perspective, helping you understand the origins of Cash Balance Plans. We trace the evolution of tax-qualified plans from their roots in mutual aid societies centuries ago, through modern pension reform efforts, ERISA and the PPA. While it's not necessary for advisors to know this history in detail, it can be helpful to have a big-picture overview of how Cash Balance Plans came to be.

8

A Brief History of Pension Plans

This chapter traces the evolution of pension plans from early mutual aid societies through pivotal historic moments that shaped today's hybrid retirement plans. Two key dates stand out in the history of Cash Balance Plans. The first is 1985, when Bank of America adopted the nation's first Cash Balance Plan, and the second is the enactment of the Pension Protection Act of 2006, which affirmed IRS approval and made the plans immune from age discrimination claims.

618 to 907

The Tang Dynasty in China forms several mutual aid societies, with members pooling together financial resources and then distributing to members in need.

1200

Medieval guilds in Europe begin to require fees from members in exchange for mutual aid, the early precursors for life insurance and pensions.

1875

The American Express Company establishes the first private pension plan in the United States.

1884

Baltimore and Ohio Railroad establishes the first pension plan by a major employer, allowing workers at age 65 with at least 10 years of service to retire and receive benefits ranging from 20% to 35% of wages.

1913

The Revenue Act of 1913, which follows the passage of the sixteenth amendment to the Constitution (permitting income taxation), recognizes the tax-exempt nature of pension trusts. At the time, several large pension trusts are already in existence, including the pension trust for ministers of the Anglican Church in the United States.

1921

The Revenue Act of 1921 exempts interest income on trusts for stock bonus or profit-sharing plans from current taxation. Trust income is taxed as it is distributed to employees only to the extent that it exceeds employees' own contributions. The Act does not authorize deductions for past service contributions.

1926

The Revenue Act of 1926 exempts income of pension trusts from current taxation.

1928

The Revenue Act of 1928 allows employers to take tax deductions for reasonable amounts paid into a qualified trust in excess of the amounts required to fund current liabilities. The Act changes the taxation of trust distributions that are attributable to employer contributions and earnings.

1929

By 1929, 397 private sector pension plans are in operation in the United States and Canada. Some major US companies that establish plans prior to 1930 are: Standard Oil of New Jersey (1903); U.S. Steel (1911); General Electric (1912); American Telephone and Telegraph (1913); Goodyear Tire and Rubber (1915); Bethlehem Steel (1923); American Can (1924); and Eastman Kodak (1929).

1935

President Franklin D. Roosevelt signs the Social Security Act.

1938

The Revenue Act of 1938 establishes the non-diversion rule to prevent pension plan assets from being diverted or used for any purpose other than the benefit of participants. The Act also makes pension trusts irrevocable.

1940

More than 4 million private sector US workers (15% of all private sector workers) are covered by a pension plan. The Investment Advisors Act of 1940 requires delegation of investment responsibilities only to an advisor registered under the Act or to a bank or an insurance company.

1942

The Revenue Act of 1942 tightens coverage standard qualifications, limits allowable deductions, and allows integration with Social Security.

1946

The United Steelworkers of America make pensions an issue in their strike against Inland Steel. At this time, the National Labor Relations Act does not cover pensions. Steelworkers Local 1010 in Indiana Harbor take the issue to the National Labor Relations Board.

1947

The Labor-Management Relations Act of 1947 (LMRA, also called the Taft-Hartley Act) provides fundamental guidelines for the establishment and operation of pension plans administered jointly by an employer and a union.

1948

The National Labor Relations Board rules that Congress intends pensions to be part of wages and that they fall under "conditions of employment" mentioned in the Act, although this is not specifically defined.

1950

General Motors (GM) establishes a pension plan for its employees. GM wants to self-fund their pension plan because they want to invest in stocks. State law prohibits insurance companies from investing pension assets in stocks. The 1950s see a bull market driven by two factors: pent-up demand after wartime restrictions are lifted, and US investment in rebuilding Europe and Japan. More than 9.8 million private sector workers (25% of all private sector workers) are covered by a pension plan.

1958

The Welfare and Pension Plan Disclosure Act of 1958 establishes disclosure requirements to limit fiduciary abuse.

1960

Approximately 18.7 million private sector workers (41% of all private sector workers) are covered by a pension plan.

1961

President John F. Kennedy creates the President's Committee on Corporate Pension Plans, prompted by growing public pressure for pension plan reform.

1962

The Welfare and Pension Plan Disclosure Act Amendments of 1962 shift responsibility for protection of plan assets from participants to the federal government to prevent fraud and poor administration.

The Self-Employed Individual Retirement Act of 1962, also known as the Keogh Act, makes qualified pension plans available to self-employed persons, unincorporated small businesses, farmers, professionals, and their employees.

1963

The Studebaker bankruptcy reveals that its pension plan was grossly underfunded. The plan is terminated, leaving thousands of employees without pensions and with no legal recourse for their pension promises. The public and many members of Congress are incensed, increasing pressure for pension plan reform. This shift ultimately leads to the passage of ERISA in 1974.

1969

The Tax Reform Act of 1969 provides fundamental guidelines for the establishment and operation of pension plans administered jointly by an employer and a union. The Act provides that part of a lump-sum distribution received from a qualified employee trust within one taxable year (on account of death or other separation from service) is given ordinary income treatment instead of the capital gains treatment it had been given under prior law. Under this Act, the bargain element on the exercise of statutory options is a tax preference item unless the stock option is disposed of in the same year the option is exercised.

1970

More than 26 million private sector workers (45% of all private sector workers) are covered by a pension plan.

1974

The Employee Retirement Income Security Act of 1974 (ERISA) is enacted. ERISA is designed to secure the benefits of participants in private pension plans through participation, vesting, funding, reporting, and disclosure rules. ERISA requires plans covering non-owner employees to provide participants with important information about plan features and funding; provides fiduciary responsibilities for those who manage and control plan assets; requires plans to establish a grievance and appeals process for participants to get benefits from their plans; and gives participants the right to sue for benefits and breaches of fiduciary duty.

ERISA also establishes the Pension Benefit Guaranty Corporation (PBGC), a form of insurance for plan participants. ERISA provides additional pension incentives for the self-employed through changes in Keoghs, and for persons not covered by pensions through individual retirement accounts (IRAs). It establishes legal status of employee stock ownership plans (ESOPs) as an employee benefit and codifies stock bonus plans under the Internal Revenue Code. It also establishes requirements for plan implementation and operation.

1975

The Tax Reduction Act of 1975 establishes the Tax Reduction Act Stock Ownership Plan (TRASOP) as an employee benefit.

1978

The dawn of the 401(k): the Revenue Act of 1978 includes section 401(k), establishing qualified deferred compensation plans under which employees are not taxed on the portion of income they elect to receive as deferred compensation rather than direct cash payments. The Act also creates simplified employee pensions (SEPs) and changes IRA rules.

1980

The Multiemployer Pension Plan Amendments Act of 1980 (MPPAA) increases multiemployer pension plan premiums and provides for payment of liability to plans for contributing employers who withdraw during the year in which the plan is less than fully funded, thereby effectively shifting primary risk of underfunding from the PBGC to contributing employers. Almost 40 million private sector workers (46% of all private sector workers) are covered by a pension plan.

1981

The Economic Recovery Tax Act of 1981 (ERTA) raises contribution limits on IRAs and Keogh plans and extends IRA eligibility to persons covered by employer pension plans. It also authorizes qualified voluntary employee contributions and permits a payroll-based tax credit instead of investment-based TRASOPs.

1982

The Tax Equity and Fiscal Responsibility Act of 1982 (TEFRA) changes Keogh plan contribution limitations, establishes a new category of plans known as top-heavy plans, and imposes more stringent sec. 415 funding and benefit limitations. It alters the provisions allowing loans to plan participants, changes rules governing integration with Social Security, reduces estate tax exclusion for proceeds of qualified retirement plans, sets age limits for plan distributions, and establishes various rules aimed at personal service corporations.

1984

The Deficit Reduction Act of 1984 (DEFRA) makes substantial changes to rules governing IRAs, SEPs, ESOPs, incentive stock options (ISOs), top-heavy plans, and golden parachutes. DEFRA freezes TEFRA's maximum annual pension benefit and contribution limits through 1987. It modifies TEFRA's top-heavy provisions and definition of key employees, and exempts government plans from top-heavy requirements. DEFRA makes changes affecting 401(k) plans, including the nondiscrimination test; substantially changes TEFRA's rules on distribution limits from qualified plans; and establishes additional tax incentives to encourage the formation of ESOPs.

The Retirement Equity Act of 1984 (REA) enhances survivor annuity rules. It insulates qualified domestic relations orders (QDROs) from ERISA preemption. REA clarifies the effect of ERISA and the Internal Revenue Code's rules prohibiting plan amendments that reduce accrued benefits with respect to early retirement subsidies, lump-sum distributions, and other "ancillary" benefits.

1985

Cash Balance Plans are first approved by the Internal Revenue Service in 1985. Bank of America is the first to introduce the Cash Balance Plan, with industry heavyweights including AT&T, IBM and Coca Cola among the hundreds of other companies that eventually embrace the hybrid pension plan. Since then, a growing number of companies have adopted this new form of pension.

Meanwhile, the Consolidated Omnibus Budget Reconciliation Act of 1985 (COBRA), included in the Single-Employer Pension Plan Amendments Act of 1986, significantly restricts the definition of insured termination for purposes of PBGC coverage. It also raises the employer's annual PBGC premium rate.

1986

The Tax Reform Act of 1986 establishes faster minimum vesting schedules, changes rules for the integration of private pension plans with Social Security, and mandates broader and more comparable minimum coverage of rank-and-file employees. It also restricts 401(k) salary reduction contributions, tightens nondiscrimination rules, and requires inclusion of all after-tax contributions to defined contribution plans as annual additions under section 415 limits.

The Omnibus Budget Reconciliation Act of 1986 (OBRA '86) requires that employers with pension plans provide pension accruals or allocations for employees who work beyond age 64 and for newly hired employees who are within five years of normal retirement age.

1987

The Omnibus Budget Reconciliation Act of 1987 (OBRA '87) changes funding rules governing underfunded and overfunded pension plans and PBGC premium levels and structure. It increases per-participant premiums for single-employer defined benefit plans and establishes a variable rate surcharge for underfunded plans. It establishes a maximum funding limit of 150% of current liability, beyond which employer contributions are not deductible. It tightens minimum funding requirements for underfunded plans and requires a quarterly premium payment for single-employer plans. It amends the Age Discrimination in Employment Act (ADEA) and ERISA to require full pension service credits for participants employed beyond normal retirement age.

1988

The Technical and Miscellaneous Revenue Act of 1988 increases the excise tax on excess pension assets on termination.

1989

The Omnibus Budget Reconciliation Act of 1989 (OBRA '89) partially repeals the interest exclusion on ESOP loans. It imposes mandatory Labor Department civil penalties on violations by qualified plan fiduciaries and creates a tax penalty for substantial overstatement of pension liabilities in determining deductibility. In addition, it requires that various forms of deferred compensation be included in the determination of average compensation and, in turn, the Social Security taxable wage base.

The firm Louis Kravitz & Associates (now Kravitz, Inc.) creates its first Cash Balance Plan when it helps a steel company convert its defined benefit plan. Kravitz, Inc. goes on to become the industry leader by creating more than 300 Cash Balance plans over the next two decades.

1990

Approximately 39.5 million private sector workers (43% of all private sector workers) are covered by a pension plan.

The Omnibus Budget Reconciliation Act of 1990 (OBRA '90) increases the excise tax on asset reversions from 15% to 20% in certain cases. It increases the excise tax to 50% if the employer does not maintain a qualified replacement plan or provide certain pro rata increases. It allows the limited use of qualified transfers of excess pension assets to a 401(h) account to fund current retiree health benefits. And it raises the PBGC flat premium and increases the variable premium.

The Older Workers Benefit Protection Act of 1990 amends the Age Discrimination in Employment Act (ADEA) to apply to employee benefits. It restores and codifies the equal-benefit-for-equal-cost principal, and sets a series of minimum standards for waivers of rights under ADEA in early retirement situations.

1992

The Unemployment Compensation Amendments of 1992 imposes a 20% mandatory withholding tax on lump-sum distributions that are not rolled over into qualified retirement accounts, liberalizes rollover rules, and requires plan sponsors to transfer eligible distributions directly to an eligible plan if requested by the participant.

1993

The Pension Annuitants Protection Act of 1993 clarifies that, in cases where a pension plan fiduciary purchases insurance annuities in violation of ERISA rules, a court may award appropriate relief, including the purchase of backup annuities, to remedy the breach.

1993

On September 3, 1993, the US Department of the Treasury issues final 401(a) (4) regulations (Income Tax Regulations 1.401(a) (4)). Section 1.401(a) (4)-8(c) of those regulations creates a "Safe Harbor" for Cash Balance Plans.

1994

The Uruguay Round Agreements Act of 1994 includes provisions from the Retirement Protection Act of 1993 to require greater contributions to underfunded plans. It limits the range of interest rate and mortality assumptions used to establish funding targets, phases out the variable rate premium cap, modifies certain rules relating to participant protections, and requires private companies with underfunded pension plans to notify PBGC before engaging in a large corporate transaction. It slows pension cost-of-living adjustments and extends through the year 2000 a tax provision that allows excess pension plan assets in certain defined benefit plans to be transferred into a 401(h) retiree health benefits account.

1996

On January 18, 1996, Notice 96-8 is published providing "Safe Harbor" interest rates for Cash Balance Plans.

The Small Business Job Protection Act of 1996 creates the savings incentive match plan for employees (SIMPLE) for small establishments. It creates a new nondiscrimination safe harbor, repeals sec. 415(e) limits, creates a new definition of highly compensated employees, modifies plan distribution rules, repeals family aggregation rules, makes USERRA technical changes, and requires that sec. 457 plan assets be held in trust.

The "Source Tax" Repeal of 1996 amends the Internal Revenue Code to eliminate state taxation of pension income received by individuals who no longer reside in the state where they earned their pensions.

Kravitz, Inc. creates its first Cash Balance Plan for a law firm. Over the next decade, the company will design and implement Cash Balance Plans for more than 100 law firms across the country. Kravitz is able to pass IRS nondiscrimination tests by demonstrating that Cash Balance Plans substantially increase retirement savings for employees as well as owners.

1999

According to one survey, 19% of Fortune 1000 firms sponsor Cash Balance Plans, and more than half of them have been established within the previous five years (US General Accounting Office, 2000).

2003

Several major Cash Balance Plans that were converted from traditional defined benefit plans are in litigation or seeking declaratory judgments over such issues as rate of accrual, whipsaw issues, and age discrimination. These plans include Bank of Boston, Xerox, IBM, and CBS. Another study concludes that Cash Balance Plans now hold more than 40% of all defined benefit pension assets.

In the summer of 2003, the Seventh Circuit in Berger v. Xerox Corp. Retirement Plan, decides that the lump sum calculation for workers terminating service prior to retirement who are covered by the defendant Cash Balance Pension Plan cannot violate the rules for defined benefit plans. In a district court in Illinois, Cooper v. IBM Personal Pension Plan decides that the very design of the Cash Balance Plan—the issue that the Campbell court only reached in dicta—has indeed violated the age discrimination rules because the "rate of benefit accruals" did "decrease" on account of the "attainment of any age."

The Lump Sum cases all hold that because Cash Balance Plans are defined benefit plans, they have to abide by the rules for defined benefit plans when the employer calculates the lump sum actuarial present value by first accruing the account balance to normal retirement age and then converting the account balance at retirement age into a life annuity before then discounting back to the current date.

2004

The US House of Representatives Committee on Education and the Workforce holds a hearing called, "Examining Cash Balance Pension Plans: Separating Myth from Fact." Much of the testimony given attests to the fact that when Cash Balance Plans are set up properly, they do not violate age discrimination policies. Committee chairman Rep. John Boehner of Ohio concluded, "Most courts have ruled no age discrimination occurs with Cash Balance Plans if the pay and interest credits given to older employee accounts are equal to or greater than those of younger employees. The most recent ruling on this topic, issued just last month in the Tootle case, agrees that Cash Balance Plans are not inherently age discriminatory."

2006

The Pension Protection Act of 2006 (PPA) is signed into law in August 2006 and officially affirms the legality and legitimacy of Cash Balance Plans. It also introduces changes that make the plans easier to implement and operate. The PPA makes Cash Balance Plans immune from claims of age discrimination. The new law also allows the use of a higher interest rate for calculation of lump sums, eliminating the whipsaw issue.

ENDNOTES

EBRI Databook on Employee Benefits, *updated 2010.* Much of the content of this chapter is used with permission from the Employee Benefit Research Institute and its excellent website, *www.ebri.org.*

Beller, Dan et al., ***Trends in Pensions*** (Washington, DC: US Government Printing Office, 1992)

Berry, Raymond and Grant, Thorton, "Plan Design in the Balance: Weighing the Pros and Cons of Cash Balance Plans," ***Journal of Accountancy*** (January 2009)

Burr, Barry B. "World War," ***Pensions and Investments*** (August 7, 1995)

Johnson, Richard. "Cash Balance Plans: what do they mean for retirement security?" ***National Tax Journal*** (June 2004)

9

Test Your Retirement Planning IQ: The Cash Balance Quiz

1. There are two types of qualified retirement plans. There are defined contribution plans, which include 401(k) and Profit Sharing plans, and defined benefit plans, which include:
   A. Traditional defined benefit plans
   B. Cash Balance Plans
   C. Both of the above
   D. None of the above

2. TRUE OR FALSE: A 55-year old business owner can quadruple his tax-deferred contributions by adding Cash Balance to an existing 401(k) Profit Sharing plan.

3. TRUE OR FALSE: 50% of professional service firms have 401(k) plans, but only 5% have Cash Balance Plans.

4. What exactly is a Cash Balance Plan?
   A. An ERISA tax-qualified plan
   B. "Hybrid" defined benefit plan

   C. Tax deduction, tax deferral, creditor protection plan
   D. All of the above
   E. None of the above

5. The first Cash Balance Plan was created:
   A. In 1950 by General Motors
   B. In 1985 by Bank of America
   C. In 2006 with the passage of the Pension Protection Act
   D. All of the above
   E. None of the above

6. TRUE OR FALSE: If the firm's cash flow changes, the firm has the option to freeze or amend the plan.

7. TRUE OR FALSE: The 2006 Pension Protection Act clarified the legality of Cash Balance Plans.

8. Cash Balance Plan investment options can include:
   A. Stocks, bonds and other alternative investments
   B. Cash Balance mutual funds
   C. Portfolios with an emphasis on fixed-income securities
   D. All of the above
   E. None of the above

9. The Employee Retirement Income Security Act (ERISA) was designed to secure the benefits of participants in private pension plans through participation, vesting, funding, reporting, and disclosure rules. In what year was it enacted?
   A. 1964
   B. 1974
   C. 1979
   D. 1984

10. By 1999, what percentage of Fortune 1000 firms sponsored Cash Balance Plans?
    A. 0.9%
    B. 9%
    C. 19%
    D. 29%
    E. None of the above

11. TRUE OR FALSE: A Cash Balance Plan credits the participants' accounts with earnings based on actual investment returns.

12. TRUE OR FALSE: Benefits accumulate in a Cash Balance Plan gradually over a participant's career versus a traditional defined benefit plan where benefits increase significantly in the years closer to retirement age.

13. What level of participation is required in a Cash Balance Plan with more than two eligible employees?
    A. 40% of eligible employees
    B. 50 total
    C. The lesser of A and B
    D. The greater of A and B
    E. None of the above

14. Like a defined benefit plan, a Cash Balance Plan can be:
    A. Insured by the SEC
    B. Insured by the DOL
    C. Insured by the PBGC
    D. Insured by the SPCA
    E. None of the above

15. TRUE OR FALSE: Owners/partners can choose varying contribution levels during the plan design stage of a new Cash Balance Plan.

16. Investment returns exceeding the Cash Balance Plan's guaranteed interest crediting rate (ICR) can result in which of the following?
    A. Overfunded plan subject to excise taxes
    B. Smaller tax deduction
    C. Lower contribution
    D. All of the above

17. TRUE OR FALSE: Technically, a Cash Balance Plan is not a defined benefit plan.

18. TRUE OR FALSE: Advisors should make plan sponsors aware that they are liable for the benefits promised by the plan if plan investments do not meet the required interest crediting rate (ICR).

19. TRUE OR FALSE: Cash Balance Plans only benefit the highly compensated owners of the firm without consideration for rank-and-file employees.

20. TRUE OR FALSE: Cash Balance Plans help business owners catch up with retirement savings goals because they allow significantly higher tax-deferred contributions, above and beyond the limits of 401(k) Profit Sharing plans.

Answer Key

1. There are two types of qualified retirement plans. There are defined contribution plans, which include 401(k) and Profit Sharing plans, and defined benefit plans, which include:
   A. Traditional defined benefit plans
   B. Cash Balance Plans
   C. Both of the above
   D. None of the above

   A Cash Balance Plan is a defined benefit plan, but because these plans also have characteristics of a defined contribution plan, they are frequently called "hybrid pension plans."

2. TRUE OR FALSE: A 55-year old business owner can quadruple his tax-deferred contributions by adding Cash Balance to an existing 401(k) Profit Sharing plan.

   TRUE—*The examples in Chapters 2 and 3 of this book, and the Contributions Limits table in Chapter 7 help make this point clear.*

3. TRUE OR FALSE: 50% of professional service firms have 401(k) plans, but only 5% have Cash Balance Plans.

   TRUE—*This fact highlights an excellent opportunity for financial advisors, since many of these firms could benefit greatly from adding Cash Balance to their existing 401(k). See Checklist #1 in Chapter 10 for examples of the best candidates for Cash Balance Plans.*

4. What exactly is a Cash Balance Plan?
   A. An ERISA tax-qualified plan
   B. "Hybrid" defined benefit plan
   C. Tax deduction, tax deferral, creditor protection plan
   D. All of the above
   E. None of the above

Companies adopt Cash Balance Plans for many reasons, including tax benefits, accelerated retirement savings, better employee benefits, and asset protection.

5. The first Cash Balance Plan was created:

   A. In 1950 by General Motors

   B. In 1985 by Bank of America

   C. In 2006 with the passage of the Pension Protection Act

   D. All of the above

   E. None of the above

   Bank of America was the first to introduce a Cash Balance Plan in 1985. Industry heavyweights including AT&T, IBM and Coca Cola are among the hundreds of companies that eventually embraced the hybrid pension plan. Today Cash Balance Plans are also increasingly popular for small businesses—80% of all Cash Balance Plans are in place at firms with fewer than 100 employees.

6. TRUE OR FALSE: If the firm's cash flow changes, the firm has the option to freeze or amend the plan.

   TRUE—*The key amendment deadline is the date before any employee has worked 1,000 hours. Amending or freezing the plan requires advance notification to participants: 15 days for plans with less than 100 lives and 45 days for plans with 100 or more lives.*

7. TRUE OR FALSE: The 2006 Pension Protection Act clarified the legality of Cash Balance Plans.

   TRUE—*The Pension Protection Act of 2006 stated that the flat percentage of salary or fixed-dollar benefit accrual type plans are not inherently age discriminatory. The PPA also approved the use of various types of interest rates for calculation of lump sums, eliminating a "whipsaw" effect.*

8. Cash Balance Plan investment options can include:

   A. Stocks, bonds and other alternative investments

   B. Cash Balance mutual funds

C. Portfolios with an emphasis on fixed-income securities

D. All of the above

E. None of the above

While there are many options, remember that the investment strategy for a Cash Balance Plan is very different from that of a 401(k) Profit Sharing plan or traditional defined benefit pension plan. Using the same principles to manage Cash Balance Plan assets that are used in managing defined contribution plan assets can spell disaster. Please review Chapter 4 for a helpful overview of key investment principles for Cash Balance Plans.

9. The Employee Retirement Income Security Act (ERISA) was designed to secure the benefits of participants in private pension plans through participation, vesting, funding, reporting, and disclosure rules. In what year was it enacted?

A. 1964

B. 1974

C. 1979

D. 1984

The Employee Retirement Income Security Act of 1974 (ERISA) is a federal law that sets minimum standards to provide protection for participants in most voluntarily established private pension and health plans.

10. By 1999, what percentage of Fortune 1000 firms sponsored Cash Balance Plans?

A. 0.9%

B. 9%

C. 19%

D. 29%

E. None of the above

According to a US General Accounting Office survey in 2000, 19% of Fortune 1000 firms sponsored Cash Balance Plans, and more than half of them had been established within the previous five years.

11. TRUE OR FALSE: A Cash Balance Plan credits the participants' accounts with earnings based on actual investment returns.

    FALSE—*Cash Balance Plans establish and credit individual accounts with income based on a predetermined formula (the "guaranteed interest crediting rate" or ICR), regardless of actual investment return. This is one of many advantages of Cash Balance Plans to non-owner employees in a firm. This issue is discussed in more detail in Chapter 4 of this book.*

12. TRUE OR FALSE: Benefits accumulate in a Cash Balance Plan gradually over a participant's career versus a traditional defined benefit plan where benefits increase significantly in the years closer to retirement age.

    TRUE—*This is why Cash Balance Plans are referred to as "hybrids." They look like a defined contribution plan in terms of crediting annual contributions, but they also credit a guaranteed rate of interest like a traditional defined benefit plan.*

13. What level of participation is required in a Cash Balance Plan with more than two eligible employees?

    A. 40% of eligible employees

    B. 50 total

    C. The lesser of A and B

    D. The greater of A and B

    E. None of the above

    For example, if a company has 30 eligible employees and chooses 12 to participate, the plan will meet Minimum Participation requirements. The plan covers the lesser of 40% of eligible employees (12) and 50 participants. The topics of Minimum Participation requirements and compliance testing are covered in Chapter 6.

14. Like a defined benefit plan, a Cash Balance Plan can be:
    A. Insured by the SEC
    B. Insured by the DOL
    C. Insured by the PBGC
    D. Insured by the SPCA
    E. None of the above

    Cash Balance Plans are insured by the Pension Benefit Guaranty Corporation (PBGC), and the employer must pay premiums. An important exception is made for plans maintained by professional service organizations (legal, medical, finance, architecture, engineering, etc.) covering 25 or fewer active participants. PBGC coverage is discussed in greater detail at the end of Chapter 6.

15. TRUE OR FALSE: Owners/partners can choose varying contribution levels during the plan design stage of a new Cash Balance Plan.

    TRUE—*This is one of the many appealing features of Cash Balance Plans for medical groups, law firms and other multi-partner/multi-owner businesses. During the plan design stage, different contribution amounts can be set for each participating partner.*

16. Excess investment returns (exceeding the Cash Balance Plan's guaranteed interest crediting rate or ICR) can result in which of the following?
    A. Overfunded plan subject to excise taxes
    B. Smaller tax deduction
    C. Lower contribution
    D. All of the above

    If the investments have outperformed the ICR, the excess return must be both recognized and realized the following year. That means reduced contribution amounts and smaller tax deductions for owners, which can defeat the purpose of having a Cash Balance Plan. If a plan is overfunded in the year that it terminates, an excise tax of approximately 50% of that excess will be applied.

17. TRUE OR FALSE: Technically, a Cash Balance Plan is not a defined benefit plan.

    FALSE—*In technical terms, it is a defined benefit plan with characteristics of a defined contribution plan.*

18. TRUE OR FALSE: Advisors should make plan sponsors aware that they are liable for the benefits promised by the plan if plan investments do not meet the required interest crediting rate (ICR).

    TRUE—*Plan sponsors are essentially promising a rate of return on balances, as defined by the ICR in the plan document. If that rate is not met, the company must contribute additional funds to make up the shortfall. That's why Cash Balance Plans require a unique investment strategy designed to meet a very specific annual objective—plan assets are marked-to-market at the end of each year. Please review Chapter 4 for a greater understanding of Cash Balance investment strategy and solutions.*

19. TRUE OR FALSE: Cash Balance Plans only benefit the highly compensated owners of the firm without consideration for rank and file employees.

    FALSE—*In order for highly compensated owners to receive significant Cash Balance Plan benefits, the plan sponsor must give meaningful benefits to employees. In fact, research shows that non-highly compensated employees typically realize a 100% increase in company contributions if their employer adopts a Cash Balance Plan. Contributions to non-HCEs are usually in the range of 5% to 8% of pay, often through an existing Profit Sharing Plan. See Myth #6 in Chapter 5 for a more in-depth look at this issue.*

20. TRUE OR FALSE: Cash Balance Plans help business owners catch up with retirement savings goals because they allow significantly higher tax-deferred contributions, above and beyond the limits of 401(k) Profit Sharing plans.

    TRUE—*The catch-up factor is one of the appeals of Cash Balance Plans, in addition to tax savings, employee retention and asset protection.*

How did you score?

If you answered more than 5 of these 20 questions incorrectly, you may want to take some time to review the previous chapters. Remember, Cash Balance Plans are not an "off-the-shelf" product and are very different from 401(k) plans. It takes time to build a solid understanding of how these plans work, from design and compliance issues to key investment principles.

Keep in mind that the time you invest today in learning about Cash Balance Plans will pay off significantly when you're able to introduce the concept to clients and prospects. When you're in the boardroom showing business owners how much they can save on taxes and how fast their retirement accounts can grow, you'll stand far above competitors who know little or nothing about the retirement industry's best-kept secret.

10

Seven Checklists to Help You Succeed

We've gathered a variety of helpful checklists to guide you as you begin marketing and selling Cash Balance Plans. Remember that the sales cycle for a Cash Balance Plan can be longer and more intensive than for an off-the-shelf 401(k), so you'll want to spend your time wisely.

The first three checklists will help you screen and evaluate prospects to make sure they're appropriate candidates. The next three checklists will help you sharpen your marketing message and close sales, and the final checklist will help you find the right actuarial firm to help your clients succeed.

✓ Checklist #1:

Top 10 Candidates for Cash Balance Plans

A Cash Balance Plan may be ideal for a company that falls into any of the following categories:

1. **Highly profitable companies of all types and sizes**
    - Usually indicated by the owner's desire for a larger tax deduction
    - Principals earning more than $250,000 per year

2. **Family businesses**
    - A Cash Balance Plan can be used as a component of succession planning

3. **Closely-held businesses**
    - Several owners want a greatly enhanced retirement plan

4. **Law firms of all sizes**
    - Tax deferral and asset protection are often very important to this profession, along with a highly competitive retirement package to help attract and retain top talent.

5. **Medical groups of all sizes**
    - Tax deferral and accelerated retirement savings make Cash Balance Plans attractive to this profession. Specialty medical groups, such as radiologists, cardiologists, and anesthesiologists, are particularly good candidates for Cash Balance Plans.

6. **Professional services firms of all types**
    - CPAs
    - Engineers
    - Architects
    - Financial Services
    - Management Consultants

7. **Older owners who have delayed saving for retirement**
    - They need to squeeze 20 years of saving into 10

8. **Firms that highly value asset protection**
    - ERISA protects Cash Balance Plan assets (and assets of all qualified retirement plans) from creditors in the event of a bankruptcy or lawsuit

9. **Those who want an enhanced benefits package to attract and retain talent**
    - They want to attract and retain high caliber employees

10. **Sole proprietorships with income exceeding $250,000 per year**

✓ Checklist #2:

Three Client Types That Benefit Most from a Cash Balance Plan

These types of clients will likely benefit the most from a Cash Balance Plan:

1. **Companies already contributing 3% to 4% of pay to employees, or at least willing to do so.** In order to pass IRS nondiscrimination testing, employers normally provide a minimum contribution of between 5% and 7.5% of salary for staff, either within the Cash Balance Plan or through a separate 401(k) Profit Sharing plan. Companies already making a 3% or higher contribution to staff within an existing retirement plan typically see a great benefit from Cash Balance.

2. **Partners or owners over 40 who want to contribute more than $49,000 per year to their retirement accounts.** Many professionals and entrepreneurs neglect personal retirement savings while building a practice or company. Adding a Cash Balance Plan allows them to rapidly accelerate retirement savings with annual pre-tax contributions from $100,000 to $200,000 or more, depending on their ages. Maximum contribution amounts allowed in Cash Balance Plans are age-dependent. The older the participants, the faster they can accelerate their retirement savings.

3. **Companies that have demonstrated consistent profit patterns.** Because a Cash Balance Plan is a qualified pension plan with required annual contributions, consistent cash flow and profit is very important. Companies should be able to maintain the committed contribution levels for at least three years.

✓ Checklist #3:

Five Critical Pieces of Information to Gather

The more you understand about a prospect's company, organizational structure and current retirement program, the better your chances of selling a Cash Balance Plan. The "Advisor Checklist" we provide in Chapter 7 is also a helpful tool. When you're ready to discuss the specifics of how a Cash Balance Plan might benefit a prospect, you'll want to gather the following five pieces of information:

1. **Company Structure**
   - Obtain as much information about the company as possible in order to help your actuarial partner determine whether this is a viable Cash Balance prospect.
   - Ask about the type of company entity, years in business, cash flow, profitability, number of employees, number of owners/shareholders/partners, and number of highly compensated employees (those earning more than $110,000 per year).

2. **Ownership Structure**
   - Obtain information about the number of equity versus non-equity shareholders or partners.
   - Find out the ages of the owners and whether any direct relatives (spouses, children, grandchildren, or parents) of the owners work for the company.
   - Try to determine when they typically file their company tax return and whether or not the company, or any of the partners/shareholders, own other businesses.

3. **Employee Demographics**
    - An ideal candidate has a number of employees younger than the owners/partners. A census should be able to provide you with most of the information that you need here. Feel free to contact us at (877) CB-Plans for a sample census request form.
    - Seek to determine if there is any group that the owners would like to include or exclude, if it were permissible.

4. **Current Plan Design**
    - The best way to get an understanding of the existing retirement program is to obtain a copy of the current plan document or Summary Plan Description, if available.
    - If the plan document is not available, try to determine if there is an employer match or Profit Sharing contribution in place. Remember, good candidates are already contributing (or willing to contribute) at least 3% of pay to employees.
    - Determine if the current plan is a Safe Harbor plan and if so, whether it's a Safe Harbor Match or 3% of Pay Safe Harbor contribution.

5. **Current Retirement Plan Administration Team**
    - Gather information about the current retirement plan team providing services to the prospective client: this may include a third-party administrator (TPA) firm, a 401(k) vendor, an existing investment advisor relationship, a CPA or other service providers.
    - Determine whether there are any service or design issues plaguing the plan. These issues or problems are your opening to offer a superior solution.
    - Find out who the key decision-makers are when it comes to retirement planning. Some large firms have a retirement committee, while in other firms an owner or managing partner may make the decisions.

✓ Checklist #4:

The 10 Biggest Retirement Planning Mistakes Clients Make

Every client is unique, but groups of clients fall into patterns of errors when it comes to retirement planning. Are your clients and prospects making some of these common mistakes? We compiled this helpful "Top 10" list through two decades of research, while designing Cash Balance Plans for more than 300 clients of all sizes and industry categories.

Revisit Chapter 1 to review these errors in detail and to understand how Cash Balance Plans can help you deliver a customized solution. The number following each item on the list indicates what percentage of companies were making this error:

1. *Relied on bad advice about IRS 401(k) rules.* (15%)
2. *Left retirement plan decisions to HR executives.* (15%)
3. *Resisted spending money to set up a tax-efficient plan.* (17%)
4. *Overestimated their own ability to handle investments.* (18%)
5. *Feared any plan that gave more money to employees.* (26%)
6. *Thought pre-tax savings were not as beneficial as after-tax savings.* (29%)
7. *Kept all assets tied up in the business.* (31%)
8. *Assumed that advanced plans were too good to be true.* (35%)
9. *Thought the IRS qualified plan limit was $16,500.* (38%)
10. *Started saving for retirement too late, or didn't save enough.* (49%)

✓ Checklist #5:

The Top Five Advantages of Cash Balance Plans

1. **Reducing taxes**

   Funds contributed to Cash Balance Plans are tax-deductible, and the earnings grow tax-deferred until the money is withdrawn. This benefit is enormous and can have a dramatic impact on savings accumulation. At retirement or when leaving employment, a Cash Balance account can be rolled into an IRA and no taxes are due until age 70½, at which point only a very small portion of the money is taxed.

2. **Accelerating retirement savings**

   Business owners and partners can often more than double their annual pre-tax retirement savings when a Cash Balance Plan is added to a 401(k) Profit Sharing plan. Many find they can squeeze 20 years of retirement savings into 10.

3. **Attracting and retaining top talent**

   Like all qualified plans, Cash Balance Plans require contributions to non-owner employees, a requirement that becomes a key benefit for many firms. Money that would otherwise have gone to the IRS is now enriching both the employer's and employees' retirement savings, helping attract, reward and retain talented employees. Professional services firms find Cash Balance Plans a great incentive on both the partner level and employee level.

4. **Shelter from creditors**

   Assets in a Cash Balance Plan are protected from creditors in the event of a bankruptcy or lawsuit. In volatile economic times, preserving profits from both taxes and creditors is increasingly important.

5. **Protecting retirement savings from market volatility**

   Because investments are usually tied to a conservative benchmark such as the 30-year Treasury rate, Cash Balance Plans have avoided the dramatic fluctuations seen in 401(k) accounts over the past few years. While 401(k) account holders often rely on higher risk strategies to maximize growth, Cash Balance Plans grow primarily through high contribution amounts earning interest rates that stay ahead of inflation without taking on major risk.

✓ Checklist #6:

Three Key Tax Benefits of Cash Balance Plans

Tax deductions are hard to come by, especially those that directly reduce ordinary income dollar for dollar. You may want to mention these tax benefits in your presentations to clients who are considering Cash Balance Plans:

1. **Business tax savings.** Cash Balance Plans are a type of "qualified plan," indicating their IRS tax-favored status. All contributions on behalf of employees are fully tax deductible. Tax advisors generally agree that qualified retirement plans should be funded to their maximum before other tax-efficient strategies are explored.

2. **Personal income tax savings for business owners and partners.** Contributions to Cash Balance Plans have the same tax effect as any deduction that reduces ordinary income dollar for dollar. With Cash Balance contribution limits as high as $100,000 to $200,000 (depending on age), many business owners can save $100,000 or more on their personal tax returns.

3. **Tax-sheltered growth of retirement funds.** With combined Federal and State income tax rates as high as 45%, the long-term tax benefits of a Cash Balance Plan are very significant. Contributions and interest credit earnings with compounding growth are sheltered from taxes until the money is withdrawn. For example, a single contribution of $130,000 earning 5% a year would be worth $561,852 at the end of 30 years. If that same $130,000 amount had been invested after taxes and if subsequent earnings on this contribution had also been taxed annually (assuming the highest tax rates indicated above), then at the end of 30 years the total value would be only $293,358; 52% of the amount calculated above.

✓ Checklist #7:

Six Questions to Ask When Choosing An Actuarial Partner

The success of a Cash Balance Plan in meeting your client's financial goals depends on creative plan design and effective plan administration. Do your due diligence before partnering with a pension actuary. You may want to ask colleagues and vendors you trust for referrals. Then use these six questions to help make a final choice:

1. **How many Cash Balance Plans do you currently administer?** If the company doesn't handle many plans, they may not have the experience to design and manage your client's plan successfully.

2. **What industries are your Cash Balance clients in?** Plan design issues and challenges vary by industry, so it's best to find a firm that successfully manages Cash Balance Plans in your client's industry. For example, law firms often have multiple tiers of participation and require an understanding of managing partnership risk.

3. **What is the size of the typical plan you handle?** A small firm's Cash Balance Plan is far simpler to manage than one with multiple partners or shareholders.

4. **How many actuaries do you have on staff?** Some firms that administer Cash Balance Plans outsource the actuarial work since they don't have an in-house actuarial team. For reasons of accountability and direct access to expertise, it's preferable to work with a specialized firm whose staff actuaries are highly experienced with Cash Balance Plans.

5. **What do your fees cover?** Ask for a detailed breakdown, and be wary of hidden fees. Also be careful of very low fees and underbidding. Cheap retirement plans become shockingly expensive when they

run into compliance and funding problems and need to be terminated or taken over by a more experienced actuary.

6. **Do you have any references I can call regarding your work on Cash Balance Plans?** A good pension actuary will happily provide client references you can call, specifically Cash Balance clients in your industry.

What's Next for Financial Advisors?

Armed with these checklists and the knowledge you've gained from reading this book, you're ready to start introducing Cash Balance Plans to your clients. Whether they have an existing 401(k) plan or they're just starting to plan a corporate retirement program, you'll be able to show them how to maximize contributions, accelerate savings, reduce taxes, and reward employees

In addition to all the marketing suggestions in Chapter 7, we've compiled "Resources from Kravitz" in the next section of this book, outlining the ways in which we can help you grow your business. From high impact Cash Balance illustrations to webinars, conference call support and coaching, we're here to help you succeed.

Resources from Kravitz

Since 1977, Kravitz has brought its clients the latest in design, administration, and management of corporate retirement plans. We have been the national leader in Cash Balance Plans since 1989. Our expert staff of 75 includes 10 actuaries and many other highly skilled technical professionals. We manage more than 1,200 retirement plans across the country, helping more than 150,000 people retire successfully.

This book represents our commitment to educating financial advisors and retirement professionals about the single most powerful tool available for accelerating retirement savings, reducing taxes and improving employee benefits. Cash Balance Plans are often called "the retirement industry's best-kept secret." We don't want them kept secret any longer, since too many business owners and their employees are missing out on the potential benefits. As you begin to grow your business with Cash Balance Plans, we invite you to take full advantage of the many resources we offer.

Presentations and Workshops

The authors of this book, Daniel Kravitz, Ken Guidroz, and Steven Sansone, are nationally recognized speakers on a wide range of retirement plan topics, including Cash Balance Plans. They are available to speak at conventions, conferences, professional association meetings and other events. Our team can customize a presentation based on the material in this book, tailored to your group's needs and interests. Learn more by visiting *www.CashBalanceBook.com*.

Customized Webinars

We frequently conduct webinars on Cash Balance Plans and other retirement planning topics. Some are available on our website, *www.CashBalanceDesign.com,* and others require registration. We can also customize a webinar to meet your organization's needs. Call (877) CB-Plans or email seminar@kravitzinc.com.

Cash Balance Illustrations

We produce easy-to-understand, high impact Cash Balance illustrations to show your clients or prospects their potential retirement plan contributions and tax savings. We require only basic employee census information. There is no cost, and turnaround time is usually less than 72 hours. Call (877) CB-Plans or send your request to email@kravitzinc.com.

Cash Balance Coach® Program

Our Cash Balance Coach® program offers web-based training to help advisors become certified as Cash Balance Consultants (CBC), a unique way to stand out in the crowded 401(k) marketplace. Launched in 2009, the program has already helped more than 400 financial advisors and retirement professionals across the country get into the Cash Balance business.

The four-part Webcast Series includes:

Cash Balance 101
Cash Balance 201
Cash Balance Investments
Cash Balance Sales & Marketing

Visit *www.CashBalanceDesign.com* to learn more and view a complete program syllabus.

The Cash Balance Marketing Library

Cash Balance Coach® alumni can take advantage of our members-only Marketing Library and other resources, including:

- Customizable Cash Balance PowerPoint presentations

- Co-author article support
- Research reports, articles and checklists
- Sample illustrations
- Co-branding options for printed marketing materials and the Cash Balance video
- Grip campaign schedule and marketing support

E-newsletters and Bulletins

Visit *www.CashBalanceDesign.com* to sign up for our Retirement Plan News e-newsletter and our Cash Balance Bulletin featuring updates, case studies, success stories, sales tips and other materials to help you succeed in the Cash Balance business.

Beyond the 401(k) Book Discussion Guide and Additional Material

Visit *www.CashBalanceBook.com* for supplemental materials to help you learn even more from this book. Download our free discussion guide, read articles on Cash Balance Plan design issues and strategies, and hear interviews with the authors. Check this helpful website regularly for updates on Cash Balance research, legislation and guidelines, including 2011 contribution limits.

Kravitz, Inc.

Los Angeles
15760 Ventura Blvd., Suite 910
Encino, CA 91436
(818) 995-6100

New York
One Penn Plaza, 36th Floor
New York, NY 10119
(212) 201-4120

Toll Free: (877) CB-Plans
www.CashBalanceDesign.com
email@kravitzinc.com

Satellite Offices

Atlanta • Las Vegas • Denver
Washington DC • Salt Lake City • Ann Arbor • Minneapolis • Charleston

Appendix

Questions and Answers about Cash Balance Plan Investments

Chapter 4 of this book explained the key principles and challenges involved in investing Cash Balance Plan assets. For those of you who wish to dig a little deeper, this Appendix provides detailed answers to some of the questions we field from financial advisors.

Q: What options are available for choosing a guaranteed interest crediting rate (ICR), and what are their advantages/disadvantages?

A: The ICR is selected from one of two interest crediting rate structures:

(1) ***A Yield-Based Structure:*** This choice allows the plan sponsor to select an interest crediting rate based upon the yield from a treasury bill, note or bond, of different durations. Back in 1996, the IRS was concerned that payouts from Cash Balance plans, which use a "lump sum" distribution payout, may have a different payout from traditional defined benefit plans, which uses a monthly payout structure. The variance between the two payout structures could result in higher or lower lump sum benefits than the actual account balance. This was commonly referred to as the "whipsaw" effect.

In order to allow Cash Balance plans to pay out the account balance without regard to the whipsaw issue, the IRS issued Notice 96-8, which, in effect, stated that cash balance plans could pay out a lump sum, provided that the Interest Crediting Rate did not exceed a specified amount. The IRS provided a range of options, most of them equal to the yield on Treasuries of different durations, plus an associated margin. One choice was the yield on the 30-year Treasury bond, which the industry has adopted for a number of reasons, some related to actuarial science and some for investment purposes. There are other choices available, including a flat fixed rate, with each choice having some advantages and disadvantages. *The weight of authority in the industry has settled on the 30-year Treasury bond for now.*

(2) ***A Return-Based Structure.*** This approach ties the ICR directly to the return of the underlying investment strategy and mandates that the strategy cannot exceed a range of 0% on the low end and the Corporate Bond Index on the high end (approximately 7% in 2010). Choosing this structure is usually an attempt to eliminate the significant consequences to the plan sponsor for underperforming a yield-based ICR. In theory, a return-based ICR removes that risk, as long as the return remained within the acceptable range. However, this is easier said than done, since Cash Balance Plan investments still need to outperform inflation, at a minimum, if they are going to appeal at all to the owners contributing significant sums of money into these accounts. Staying within the acceptable range in all types of economic and market cycles could be exceptionally challenging.

As of the first quarter of 2010, we are unaware of any plan using a return-based ICR structure receiving a Favorable Determination Letter (FDL) from the IRS and are hopeful that the anticipated upcoming regulations will provide more guidance on this issue in particular.

Q: Can the ICR be changed?

A: Once written into the plan document, the guaranteed interest crediting rate can only be changed prospectively to new contributions, not retroactively to benefits already accrued in the plan at the time of the change. Doing so would change the benefit promised to the plan participant and thus violates IRS regulations.

Q: If all a plan sponsor needs to do is match the 30-year Treasury bond yield, why not just go out and purchase the 30-year Treasury bond, laddering them over the years?

A: That strategy wouldn't work because of the inverse relationship between the price of a bond and its yield. As interest rates rise, the price of the bond will fall in value and vice versa. Assuming that the 30-year Treasury bond has an average duration of 12 years or so, a 1% rise in interest rates would result in a 12% decline in the value of the bond, offset by the income produced on the bond. Assuming a 5% yield, the client would net out a –7% total return. If the plan's interest crediting rate was 3% in 2009, for example, the plan would have a shortfall of approximately 10%. On a $5 million Cash Balance Plan, that's $500,000 that the plan sponsor (partners, shareholders, etc.) would need to come up with in order to attain fully funded status. And that's in addition to their contributions for the year. It just doesn't work.

Q: What time horizons are involved in Cash Balance Plan investing, and how do they drive investment strategy?

A: There are three distinct investment horizons at play in a Cash Balance Plan:

(1) The plan assets must be "marked to market" by the actuarial team at the end of every plan year. An investment strategy structured for longer than a one-year horizon could get caught in the wrong cycle and decimate plan assets. Unlike other types of pension plans where

investment managers can average out their returns over three, five, 10 years or longer, the ICR must be hit each year.

(2) The second investment horizon for the Cash Balance Plan concerns plan participants. These plans are designed to fund a benefit at the maximum level over a 10 to 12 year period. In addition, participants may be able to have in-service withdrawals starting at age 62. Those two factors tell you right away that the investment strategy has to be structured differently than a personal investment strategy or a longer term 401(k) strategy.

(3) The third and final investment horizon is duration of the sponsoring entity itself. Partnerships dissolve and partners leave all the time. If the plan is underfunded when either of these events occur, no money is paid out to the partners until the plan is restored to fully funded status by paying the shortfall in full. And since this could happen at any time, the investment advisor should structure the strategy accordingly, with a conservative approach focused on capital preservation, meeting the ICR annually to prevent any shortfalls.

Q: What happens if plan investments don't meet the ICR by the end of the plan year?

A: When investments fail to meet the guaranteed interest crediting rate for a particular plan year, the shortfall can be dealt with in one of two ways. One option is for the plan sponsor to "pay in full," covering the shortfall by the time the tax return is filed. That option will keep the plan in a fully funded status. The second option is to amortize the loss over a period of seven years, in an effort to smooth out the funding level. This latter option is not a free pass, rather, it helps plan sponsors mitigate the severe financial impact by spreading the funding payments over time.

When a plan is in an underfunded status, certain benefit restrictions and requirements kick into place. Employee notifications are required and the IRS will mandate quarterly (rather than annual) contributions. Payments to owners and highly compensated employees may be restricted, and if the funding level is classified as "distressed," the plan is frozen and no benefits or payouts are allowed. Most firms do not wish to remain in an underfunded status for very long, not to mention the cash flow issues described below.

Q: Why is it so important that Cash Balance Plans remain fully funded at all times?

A: IRS regulations are such that underfunding creates a significant amount of pressure on the firm's cash flow. An aggressive investment strategy can create serious problems. For example, a 10% loss in one plan year, coupled with a guaranteed interest crediting rate of 5% requires the plan sponsor to come up with 15% in that particular year, regardless of the economic circumstances or firm cash flow. On a $2 million plan, that's a $300,000 required contribution; on a $20 million plan, that's a $3,000,000 contribution. A 30% loss creates an immediate $600,000 liability for the $2 million plan and an immediate $6 million liability for the $20 million plan. As mentioned above, losses can be amortized over a seven-year period, but this results in numerous IRS restrictions and requirements, including the possibility of the plan being frozen.

Q: What are the consequences for outperforming the ICR?

A: When the investment strategy results in gains that exceed the guaranteed interest crediting rate, these gains must be recognized in the following plan year. The consequences for such an action are as follows:

(1) ***Reduced Tax Deduction.*** The excess amount will be used in the following year's calculation to determine the owners' contribution amounts. It will most likely result in a reduced contribution and reduced tax deduction for them. If a key objective of the plan is to maximize tax deductions for high wage earning owners or partners,

the investment strategy that delivered excess returns is out of alignment. It also subjects the plan to a level of risk that could very well result in a year of underperformance.

(2) ***Excise Tax.*** If a plan is overfunded in the year that it terminates, an excise tax of approximately 50% of that excess will be applied. In effect, the reward to the owner for taking that extra investment risk and receiving less of a tax deduction is a 50% penalty tax.

Q: Can excess returns (above the ICR) be amortized over a number of years like plan losses?

A: No, there is no smoothing allowed for excess returns. The net effect of excess returns is to lower the amount of allowable contributions for the owners/partners. While this seems like a good problem to have, it is still a problem. Remember that the plan was established to provide significant contributions (tax deductions) to the owners of the company, firm or partnership. From a tax planning perspective, having contributions reduced because the investment strategy took on additional risk and outperformed the ICR (in some cases by large margins) is problematic for those counting on the deduction. It is somewhat analogous to cases in which a 401(k) plan fails IRS fairness testing, resulting in owners or other highly compensated employees having to receive refunds on their contributions. Once you're counting on the contribution and tax deduction, it is difficult to lose it, and then have to pay the taxes on the income.

Q: Is there an equity risk premium for Cash Balance Plan investments?

A: No, because equity risk is highly problematic in Cash Balance Plan investments. The equity risk premium argues that an investor should receive a certain level of return (or premium) over the risk-free rate of return at various levels of equity allocation to his or her portfolio. While we may embrace this theory in areas of personal investment, it does not work in a Cash Balance Plan. In personal investing, equity returns receive favorable tax treatments in the form of capital gains. In a Cash Balance Plan, equity gains typically lead to exceeding the ICR and reducing the allowable tax deduction, resulting in ordinary income tax or worse, 50% excise tax if the plan is terminating. The tax implications dramatically reduce the equity risk premium advantage, in our view.

Acknowledgments

We would like to express our deepest appreciation to everyone who made this book possible, starting with our valued clients. We dedicate this book to the thousands of hardworking business owners who have entrusted us with their retirement plans over the past 33 years. Their loyalty and encouragement helped Kravitz become the national Cash Balance leader and ultimately inspired us to write this book.

We also dedicate this book to our incredibly dedicated, smart and diligent Kravitz team, from actuaries and technical specialists to administrators, operations staff and client service consultants. Their expertise and creativity shaped the ideas in this book.

Special thanks to the fast-growing network of financial advisors and retirement professionals who have asked Kravitz for help bringing the advantages of Cash Balance Plans to their clients. With their encouragement, we created the Cash Balance Coach® training program in 2009, sharing our knowledge and experience with everyone who could benefit. The enthusiastic response to Cash Balance Coach® (400 alumni and counting) and the constant demand for information and marketing support motivated us to get this book published as soon as we could.

A heartfelt thanks goes to Louis Kravitz, who founded Kravitz in 1977 and designed one of the country's first successful Cash Balance Plans in 1989. An inspired leader and teacher, Lou launched us into the Cash

Balance business and continues to share his experience and insight with the whole Kravitz team.

We greatly appreciate the support of valued friends and colleagues, including Laurence Balter, Wade Behlen, David Bonifas, Jim Elliott, Marc Emmer, Todd Feltz, Tom Foster, Mick Fouts, George Fraser, Joe Frustaglio, Dennis Glynn, Brian Graff, Mitch Haber, David Hilton, Tim Hines, Don Holt, Bruce Jensen, Corbon Kinney, Rick Kirby, Mike Laney, Tom Lastuvka, Barbara Lewis, Stephen Lippman, Dr. Robert Masters, Brian Matthews, Richard May, Brian Miller, Scott Miller, Sean Miller, Stephan Miskjian, Matthew Murphy, John Nelson, Hugh O'Toole, Joan Payden, Fred Reish, David Roberts, Louis Rossie, Gary Rubin, Mike Shamburger, Steve Thomas, Jeffrey Ulmer, John Villegas, Anthony Warren, Scott Weiner, Ted Welsh, David West and so many others who have helped and inspired us along the way.

We also thank Henry deVries, our collaborator, for his experience and guidance through the process of writing and publishing this book. Thanks to Dana and Ellen Borowka for encouraging us to write the book and introducing us to Henry deVries. Special thanks to Martha Ophir for all her work editing, revising and producing the final manuscript. We are grateful to Bruce Rigney and his team at Rigney Graphics, and to Michele DeFilippo and her team at 1106 Design, for their creativity and expertise in book design.

Last but not least, we want to thank our families for all their love and support, for putting up with our long hours and for believing in us. Thanks to each and every one of you: Shelby, Tim, Alex and Jordan Kravitz; Joyce, Jess, Lucas and Chris Guidroz; Lynn, Brittany, Brooke and Stevie Sansone; and Kathy Kravitz.

About the Authors

Daniel Kravitz

Daniel Kravitz is the President of Kravitz, Inc., the largest independent firm of retirement plan consultants headquartered in California. Daniel is nationally recognized as a leading expert on Cash Balance Plans, and has been a featured speaker at numerous national retirement industry conferences. He has written more than 25 articles on Cash Balance Plans for business and professional journals and has been interviewed by the *Wall Street Journal.*

Daniel leads a team of more than 75 skilled professionals, including 10 actuaries. Under his leadership, Kravitz has expanded to serve more than 1,200 clients across the country, earning a national reputation for leading-edge retirement plan design. Daniel ensures that all divisions of Kravitz stay focused on the company's primary goal: extraordinary customer service, excellent client communications, and delivery of accurate and timely work products.

A graduate of the University of California, Davis, Daniel has earned the Certified Pension Consultant designation from the American Society of Pension Professionals & Actuaries (ASPPA). He was awarded the Martin Rosenberg Achievement Award and has served on the board of the National Institute of Pension Administrators (NIPA).

Ken Guidroz, MBA

Ken Guidroz serves as Director of New Plan Design for Kravitz. He has designed innovative Cash Balance Plans for companies throughout the country. Working in partnership with the firms' expert team of actuaries, he has helped hundreds of business owners accelerate retirement savings, reduce taxes, and enhance employee benefits.

Ken played an instrumental role in creating and launching the Kravitz Cash Balance Coach® program. He conducts many of the Coach webinars and works closely with financial advisors and retirement plan professionals, teaching them how to grow their businesses by marketing and selling Cash Balance Plans. Ken also speaks nationally on Cash Balance topics to CEO groups, trade organizations, and professional meetings of CPAs, financial advisors and financial planners.

Ken brings a broad range of business experience to Kravitz. He earned his MBA from Pepperdine University in 1995 and worked in the pharmaceutical industry for 10 years. In addition Ken has served in Christian ministry for 15 years, five of them as a senior pastor.

Steven S. Sansone, JD, AIF®

Steve Sansone is a Principal of Kravitz Investment Services, Inc., the Registered Investment Advisory affiliate of Kravitz, Inc. Steve helped create the Kravitz Cash Balance Coach® program, and has been essential to the program's growth and success. Steve is also a Co-President of Payden/Kravitz, a joint venture between Payden & Rygel and Kravitz Investment Services, and has played a key role in building distribution for the Payden/Kravitz Cash Balance Plan Fund.

Steve has more than 25 years of experience in the retirement plan industry, and is a frequent speaker at national conferences. For nearly 20 years, he worked as one of the top pension wholesalers in the industry, with Manulife Financial/John Hancock, selling over 1,000 retirement plans and being the first sales representative to bring in over $1 billion in retirement plan assets for John Hancock. Steve helped establish the National Institute of Pension Administrators (NIPA) Los Angeles Chapter and served as its President for 10 years.

Steve graduated from the State University of New York at Buffalo School of Law (Cum Laude) and serves as a member of the Board of Directors for Bank of Santa Clarita, in Santa Clarita, California.

Notes

Notes

Notes